Browns 8116 £10.99

THE REGIS STUDY SKILLS GUIDE

FIFTH EDITION

Middlesbrough College

00104455

THE REGIS STUDY SKILLS GUIDE

FIFTH EDITION

Frank Walsh

updated by Chris Reisig

International Debate Education Association

New York*Amsterdam*Brussels

Published by:

International Debate Education Association

400 West 59th Street

New York, NY 10019

Library of Congress Cataloging-in-Publication Data

Walsh, Frank, 1949-

 The Regis study skills guide / Frank Walsh ; updated by Chris Reisig.

-- 5th ed.

   p. cm.

 Includes bibliographical references and index.

 ISBN 978-1-932716-37-5 (alk. paper)

 1. Study skills. 2. Learning. I. Reisig, Chris. II. Title.

 LB1049.W26 2008

 371.3'0281--dc22

                              2007051908

Design by Gustavo Stecher and Juan Pablo Tredicce | imagenHB.com

Printed in the USA

 **IDEBATE** PRESS

Table of Contents

Introduction

Mark Twain once made the observation "Nothing so needs reforming as other people's habits." Even though it concerns the hypocrisy involved in attempting to influence the behavior of others, this remark serves to point out a basic impulse in our human nature: the impulse to provide helpful advice to those who can benefit by it. In the pages that follow, we, the creators of this text, will attempt to satisfy our urge to shape the form of your conduct, not because we are pushy, power-hungry people who seek to feed off of your time and energy, but because we believe that certain patterns of study behavior are vastly superior to others. At every stage, we have based our recommendations upon our experience and upon available scholarship in the area of study habits. Rest assured that we are not attempting to trick you into the adoption of old-fashioned and useless techniques. In fact, we have taken the time to compile this book precisely because we recognize that you are all individually talented and totally *modern* students.

As you progress through school, you will find that you have more and more freedom to achieve goals that you will choose for yourself. Never before have students had so much say in determining what direction their own education will take. But recognize that with this freedom comes an increased obligation to perform efficient independent study. As the great playwright, George Bernard Shaw, phrased the matter, "Liberty means responsibility. That is why most men dread it." This book is motivated by our desire to be your guide, not your dictator, on an educational voyage that should be welcomed and cherished, rather than dreaded. If you do not believe that this is our actual intention, then, to be quite frank, there is absolutely no point in reading beyond this line of print.

If you are still reading, let us point out to you at once a frequently forgotten fact about your education: at the higher levels, teachers teach subjects, not necessarily the most effective ways to learn those subjects. Often, they will not show you how to read more efficiently, instruct you in the development of a better memory or a better vocabulary, guide you in the processes of organizing time or notetaking, or educate you in how you should go about taking a test. Teachers and their various courses merely present you with the occasions to develop these skills—occasions that you must take advantage of yourself. You must thus devise your own method of study, founded on motives that you yourself provide, judged and monitored by your own occasional evaluations of how you are doing, and specifically designed to combat your own particular weaknesses. This may sound like a frighteningly big task, but it is worth every ounce of energy you invest in it. Once you are equipped with an appropriate method of study, or in other words, once you know *how to learn*, you will find that you do not have to force yourself to work, that you get more done in less time, and that your academic performance vastly improves.

Always remember that the overall goal of your education is, after all, to prepare or shape yourself as a lifetime learner. Twenty years from now you probably will not be called upon to remember the name of Alexander the Great's horse, the precise date of

Shakespeare's death, or that the sine of 90° is 1. But you probably will be called upon, even several decades from today, to read and absorb information rapidly, to speak intelligently, and to write clearly and effectively. While many of your courses and much of the specific information you are studying may not seem vitally important to your life now or perhaps even to your future, you must remain ever aware that they aim at one final goal: rendering you an independent learner who can succeed on his or her own in college and is prepared for whatever job he or she desires. If you can keep this long-term objective in the forefront of your mind, you will undoubtedly find it easier to do work that may be, in itself, unenjoyable and without much recognizable value.

Imagine you are stranded on a deserted island, and your one objective is to sail back to your friends and loved ones. While the isolated act of making and sharpening an axe, for example, may not itself fill you with hope of achieving your goal, it is a heartening and encouraging labor when you see it in a larger context. While you fully realize that you cannot sail home on the axe itself and that you would gain little by throwing it in the air as some sort of signal flare, you are nevertheless enthusiastic about the construction and refinement of the tool. Why? Because you are always conscious that you are developing a means or method that will ultimately enable you to achieve your final end of constructing a raft and floating off to your destination. And so it is with your work in school: you are forging your mind into a tool of sorts, ever sharpening its edge on the work you are doing for classes, never being discouraged by the occasional setbacks involved in academic life, always trying to see how individual evenings of study or particular assignments are means to achieving the overall purpose of your education.

Obviously, it is most crucial that you develop good study habits. Even if you are that exceptional student who has had the capacity to "coast" through earlier courses, you will discover that upper level college classes and graduate and professional schools pose such severe academic challenges that your lack of well-formed study habits is certain to prevent you from achieving success. Moreover, your failure to develop the proper practices now will make it more difficult, perhaps even impossible, to reverse your bad habits later.

Then, too, do not forget that for the first time in your life, you are under considerable pressures of time: the academic load has never been heavier; you may have a lengthy trip to and from school; you are committed to participation in various extracurricular activities; you want to maintain the friendships you have formed in your previous school and in your community. How can you find time to do all of the many things you want to do? The point is that, if you want to be successful in school, you are going to have to devote substantial time to private study. And since you have so many other worthwhile things to do, you want to get the most out of every minute that you are giving over to academic work. The best way to do this is to acquire a rhythm in your habits of study that makes the act itself less difficult and that frees you to devote time to all of your other interests. The purpose of this brief text is to enable you to do exactly that.

And who knows, after a while you may even come to *enjoy* studying most or all of your subjects. Like all forms of hard work, study can be very satisfying, especially when you see a high correlation between how hard you are working and your grades. You may find that the peace and security bred by academic effort are preferable to the chaos and nail-biting spawned by blind reliance on chance. You may well discover what Thomas Jefferson, a scholar of the highest order, came to realize about his own good fortune: "I'm a great believer in luck, and I find the harder I work the more I have of it."

How to Use This Book

A few brief words about the three different parts of each chapter should be sufficient to explain how this book should be used.

A. *Questions for Self-Evaluation* At the beginning of each chapter, you will find a series of questions related to the material covered in that section. You will quickly recognize that the ideal or "correct" of the three choices would be to place a check in the extreme right, "Often/Always" column. However, it is most important that you answer all questions *honestly* and as thoughtfully as you possibly can. Their purpose here is basically twofold: first, to convince you from the start that when you study now, you are not working at maximum efficiency (that is, to the best of your ability); and second, to make you better aware, by the number of boxes checked in the central and left-hand columns), of which sections of this book you personally should devote the greatest attention to mastering.

B. *Goals* Sometimes, when you are earlobe deep in alligators, you must pause to remind yourself that the initial objective was to drain the swamp. As you shall see, the format of this book is designed to keep goals and objectives at the fore. After you have completed any given section, you should return to the "Goals" presented at its beginning and ask yourself whether or not your reading of the chapter has prepared you to achieve those goals. If your answer is affirmative, move on to the next section; if it is negative, reread the chapter and consult your faculty advisor about specific difficulties with the section. Use the occurrence of such problems as opportunities to involve your teacher, faculty advisor, or counselor in a plan to improve your study habits. Many times, you will find that they can assist you in directing your energies more wisely in particular areas or subjects; and they will often have suggestions of their own to complement the ones you will find in this text.

C. *Suggestions for Improvement* The substance of this book consists of a series of observations and tips on how to improve your capabilities in various areas related to study. These numbered remarks reflect habits or procedures that many good students have found useful in improving their academic performance. However, let it be clearly stated at the outset that not every suggestion is a "pearl" that will surely make you the perfect learning machine. You are a unique person, not a machine, and your individual learning style plainly differs from the styles of others. The point, therefore, is that you should read these tips carefully, noting those observations and adopting those techniques that might have value for you. Remember, nevertheless, that some things "have to be believed in order to be seen"; give these proven suggestions a sincere try before you decide to dismiss any of them. Do not act as if ours is the powerless voice of popular opinion while you are Frederick the Great of Prussia ("My people and I have come to an agreement: they are to say what they please, and I am to do what I please"), or some other such narrow-minded governor of his own conduct. In other words, listen!

Actually, a fourth and final part of this text is missing, namely, a means of evaluating your study habits after you have tried out our suggestions. After about a month of working with the methods recommended in this book, you should go back and re-answer the self-evaluation questions at the beginning of the various sections. This simple step will enable you to determine whether you have made much of an improvement. You alone are finally responsible for bettering your study habits; evaluating your progress should really be self-initiated, or something you want to do when you decide to do it.

Chapter I

Environment and Concentration in Study

A. *Questions for Self-Evaluation*

Place a check mark in the column that you feel most accurately describes your own case now.

a. Rarely / Never

b. Sometimes

c. Often / Always

a	b	c

1. Do I study by myself rather than with others? _____ _____ _____

2. Do I study in certain regular locations? _____ _____ _____

3. Do I study in places that are relatively quiet and private? _____ _____ _____

4. Do I turn off the radio, TV, or computer when I begin to study? _____ _____ _____

5. Are desk, chair, lighting, and room temperature conditions in the places where I work good for study? _____ _____ _____

6. Do I try to get some relaxation
before I begin to study?   _____ _____ _____

7. When I begin to study, do I have a clear
grasp of my objectives?   _____ _____ _____

8. Do I plan short breaks into long,
continuous periods of study?   _____ _____ _____

9. Do I begin to study at the time I have
planned to do so?   _____ _____ _____

10. Do I study with a pencil in my hand?   _____ _____ _____

11. Am I untroubled by distractions
or daydreams when I study?   _____ _____ _____

12. When I am finished studying, do I take time
out to evaluate how successful I have been?   _____ _____ _____

B. *Goals*

When you complete this chapter, you will

1. know what two locations you should use for studying;
2. know what physical conditions in the environment are likely
to maximize your studying effectiveness;
3. be familiar with a method to help you begin to concentrate;

4. have a plan to achieve specific study objectives, as well as an evaluation procedure that will motivate and improve study;

5. be better able to control distractions and the desire to daydream.

C. *Environment and Concentration in Study*

The environment in which you study and your ability to concentrate your attention on material are two critical and interlocking factors in effective studying. For this reason, we should devote some space to observations about each.

Your Study Environment:

1. Select one place at home and one place at school that you will use only for study. If you commute back and forth to school, use the bus or the train only for glancing over less important material or for reviewing matter you have already committed to memory. (For sure, travel time can always be put to some good purpose, but you should match your use of such time to the type of task that can be accomplished reasonably well under the sometimes brutal conditions involved in transit. As the old saying goes, "When you are stuck with a lemon, make lemonade!")

2. To the extent possible, study in a place where you are unlikely to be interrupted by friends, roommates, or relatives. Always study by yourself, unless you are working with a tutor or participating in a discussion or study group that is supremely serious about the subject at hand.

3. Choose to study in a place that is relatively free from noise. Do not play a radio, mp3 player, or television in the background, because your mind has to burn additional energy to concentrate over background noise. At the same time, however, do not become excessively annoyed by extraneous sounds around you. Your emotional disturbance will have a far more damaging impact on concentration than the noise itself.

4. Unless absolutely necessary to your work, turn off your computer, as Internet surfing, email, and instant messaging can be extreme sources of distraction. Powering down your PC (or at least turning off your monitor) will help you focus on the work at hand, rather than causing one eye to stay on your homework and the other one on the screen. When you do need to use a computer (whether it be for specific research or for writing a paper), use only the programs you need and stay focused. Make sure to turn off the PC or monitor once you have completed your intended work.

5. Select a place where temperature conditions are suitable for study. As a rule, it is best to choose a location that is slightly cooler than the norm.

6. If possible, study while sitting up in a straight-back chair, as sitting erect keeps your muscles tense and your mind more alert, and at a desk that is comfortably high and faces the wall. If no desk is available, sit at a high table in the most peaceful surroundings your home, dorm room, or school can provide.

7. Place and, if possible, keep everything that you will need for work on the desk or table, and remove any and all objects that are unrelated to study.

8. If possible, study with a desk lamp that has a fluorescent light, preferably a draftsman's type with extension arms, and have an overhead light source in the room to eliminate eye-tiring shadows. Use a light-colored blotter to minimize glare.

9. When making use of a computer in your studying, position your chair so that your eyes are normally about two feet from the screen. To avoid glare and resulting eyestrain, locate the computer away from any window where natural light might fall directly onto the screen, or where daylight from behind might force you to squint.

Concentration:

1. It is always a good idea to relax as much as you can before you begin to study. In the evening, have a regular time to start studying so that you can plan a rest period immediately before.

2. Before you begin to study, get a good focus on the objectives of your work. What do you intend to accomplish? How long will it take you to accomplish it? (Thus, you should aim to read 50 pages in an hour, or to review two chapters of a text-book in 30 minutes, etc.) These aims are intended to make your mind more *active* in your learning, and they should be set according to your individual strengths and weaknesses. Always set goals that are realistic for you to attain: nothing is more damaging to your motivation to study than failure to achieve what you set out to do.

3. If you are going to study for one long, continuous period, plan a few short breaks into the time. These give you something to

look forward to and often provide valuable rest for your eyes and mind.

4. Always begin to study at the precise time you had planned to initiate work. Use some formal act to signal the start of study. (For example, you might turn on the desk lamp, turn off the radio, sharpen your pencil, etc.)

5. Keep a memo or reminder pad handy to note distracting ideas that might occur to you as you are studying. When you are finished studying, or during your planned breaks, you can follow up on these various thoughts.

6. Always keep a pencil in your hand to direct your attention to the material you are studying. If you are frequently distracted, consider using the check-mark technique for improving concentration. On every occasion that you catch yourself not concentrating, place a check mark on the memo or reminder pad beside you. The act of checking will serve as a conscious reminder for you to return to work. (At first you will probably accumulate many checks, but after a few weeks, you will accumulate very few.)

7. To keep daydreaming to a minimum, make an effort to "psyche yourself up" about the subject you are studying. If you approach your Social Studies homework with the attitude of a Henry Ford ("History is bunk!"), or your Art assignment with the bias of a Hermann Goering ("When I hear anyone talk of Culture, I reach for my revolver"), your chances of becoming interested in the material at hand are admittedly somewhat slim. Try as hard as you can to suspend your judgment of the

work's value until you have completed it, and try to postpone daydreams until your planned break.

8. When you have completed studying, review how efficiently your time was spent. Did you achieve your goal in the allowed time? Was the experience satisfying? Give some thought to how you can improve your study habits and concentration in the future. Remember that you alone are capable of and responsible for measuring how efficiently you are studying.

Chapter II

Organizing Time

A. *Questions for Self-Evaluation*

Place a check mark in the column that you feel most accurately describes your own case now.

a. Rarely / Never

b. Sometimes

c. Often / Always

a	b	c

1. Do I avoid last-minute "cramming" (studying new information for an extended length of time) before examinations?

2. Do I finish my assignments on time?

3. Do I have a sufficient amount of time for sleep and recreation?

4. Do I adapt the length of my study periods to the type and difficulty of my work?

5. Do I find time to review class notes and assigned readings before class?

6. Do I do some work in every subject on the nights I study?   _____ _____ _____

7. Before I begin to study a new chapter in a textbook, do I find time to review old material?   _____ _____ _____

8. Do I use my weekend time efficiently, spreading out the workload between Saturday and Sunday?   _____ _____ _____

9. Do I study my most difficult subjects during the time period when I work most efficiently?   _____ _____ _____

10. Do I use my study periods and unscheduled time wisely and effectively?   _____ _____ _____

11. Do I avoid studying two very similar subjects in a row?   _____ _____ _____

12. From time to time, do I stop to evaluate how effectively I am using my time?   _____ _____ _____

B. *Goals*

When you complete this chapter, you will

1. appreciate some of the advantages of using a schedule;
2. know those principles for budgeting time that will help you to create a useful schedule;
3. have a sense of how a schedule should be applied once it has been devised.

C. *Organizing Time*

Tobias Smollett, the 18th-century author of such blockbuster novels as *The Expedition of Humphrey Clinker* and *The Adventures of Peregrine Pickle*, once remarked, "Some folks are wise, and some are otherwise." Probably nothing so clearly marks a person for membership in the second of these two categories as having a disorganized approach to the use of time. Therefore, we should introduce you at once to a key element in insuring the most efficient allocation of time, namely, the schedule. The advantages to budgeting portions of your day to assigned tasks are obvious and too many in number to be discussed in great detail here. Let it be said, however, that among the numerous reasons for adopting a systematic approach to the day are the following:

1. A schedule functions as a goal: because the thing exists and is there for you to follow, you are more likely to feel an obligation to do so. Thus, a schedule can get you started studying when you otherwise would not feel the need to begin; and once under way, it can tell you whether you are proceeding

in the right direction at the right speed. In short, where your objectives are clearly defined, as they always are in a well-constructed schedule, they prove to be powerful motivating forces in themselves.

2. A schedule itself is a habit; as such, it will help to make studying, a part of your schedule, a habit. Studying becomes less and less painful when performed on a steady and consistent basis. You will probably find yourself falling into a "study rhythm" — a tide that requires increasingly less conscious willpower with which to flow.

3. A schedule guarantees that you will not neglect subjects you do not enjoy, and it promotes review and eliminates the need for last-minute cramming. These advantages stem from the fact that when you are making out a schedule, you are being more objective and reasonable about what you should do and how long it will take you to do it than at any other time.

4. A schedule guarantees the proper amount of rest and relaxation.

5. A schedule guarantees that, when you do study, you are getting the most out of your time. Operating within the "system" set up by a schedule, you *must* achieve certain results within the time allowed, or you are penalized with the loss of your free time.

6. A schedule provides satisfaction when it is properly executed, and thus provides additional incentive to continue working.

Oddly enough, however, the primary advantage in keeping to a schedule is probably that, by so doing, you actually increase your flexibility and freedom to do what you want to do when you decide to do it. If you adhere to a study schedule, you will never again have to face assignments stacked up to your eyeballs, and your time will never again be dominated by the sheer enormity of the workload. In other words, there will never again be a weekend spent closeted in your room with 52 hours of work to be performed in a possible 48.

General Observations on Making a Schedule:

1. Like Frankenstein's creation, a schedule is a relatively easy thing to put together, but once brought to life, it is a monster to control. Be prepared to make changes in your permanent schedule (if, for example, you find that a particular subject is becoming increasingly more difficult and demands more of your time), or even to break the schedule on rare occasions. Be flexible, but keep following your permanent schedule as much as possible until it becomes a habit.

2. Remember that you should not go overboard in scheduling. Do not become too specific in assigning lengths of time for study to particular subjects. Be generous in allowing time for your work. (If you plan a 25-minute study period for English and are suddenly asked to write an essay for the next class, you are in big trouble!) Adjust the lengths of time you will spend on particular subjects well in advance of the days on which you will do the work. In other words, plan for tests and papers one or two weeks in advance. But again, do not attempt to be too prophetic in this regard by planning a month

or six weeks ahead of time. Recall this observation of Winston Churchill: "It is always wise to look ahead, but difficult to look farther than you can see."

3. The pages immediately following this chapter provide two charts. Chart #1 should be used to keep a record of your time for one or two weeks. Chart #2 should be used to plot out a regular and permanent weekly schedule, based upon the typical week of classes and study recorded on Chart #1. This schedule should be re-evaluated and adjusted periodically to insure that it meets your academic and recreational needs. As you are looking over the time log kept on Chart #1 and making out your permanent schedule on Chart #2, you should ask yourself a series of questions that will have a bearing on time allocation:

   a. For which activities would you like to have more time? When can you make time?

   b. What "high payoff areas" (things that are particularly rewarding given the relatively little amount of time that need be devoted to them) do you spend too little time on now? What should you start doing now?

   c. What time-consuming and relatively useless things do you do now that you should cut down on? What should you stop doing now?

   d. At what time of the day are you most productive? What academic subjects or activities should you be engaged in during those hours?

   e. When are you least productive, creative, or effective? What should you be doing during those hours?

f. With what subjects do you foresee special difficulties? How much extra time will you need to cope with these difficulties?

g. How should you use your weekends? What percentage of the workload and what type of work should you be performing on weekends?

h. For what continuous length of time can you study without a dramatic reduction in efficiency? How much total time can you reasonably expect to study in one day?

Specific Suggestions for Making a Schedule:

1. Schedule the hours you will devote to necessary activities, such as meals, classes, a part-time job, recreation, and sleep. You should schedule yourself for at least seven or eight hours of sleep per night and about twenty hours of recreation per week. Plan to get some exercise every day; allow yourself time to view your favorite TV show, to surf the Net, or to listen to that new CD you recently purchased; and even arrange some time for playing chess or just "shooting the breeze" in the cafeteria or student lounge. (By formally planning to engage in such activities, you are providing yourself a reasonable amount of relaxation, while minimizing the possibility that you will indulge your appetite to gluttonous excess.)

2. Plan your study periods. Figure out the approximate number of hours per week that you will need to devote to each subject. Use the time log shown on Chart #1 to assess this.

3. Adapt the length of each study period to what you anticipate to be the type and difficulty of the work you will be doing. If

a subject will involve much memorizing, plan short periods of work with rest periods before and after. If you will be reading plays and novels, plan longer periods of continuous study. Textbook studying should usually be planned in periods lasting for 40 minutes to an hour, and should be followed by at least a short rest period.

4. Schedule each study period as close in time as possible to the class period it prepares you for. If you have free time following a class, review class notes and do some advanced preparation for the next class. If not, schedule time for these activities later on the same day.

5. Do some work in each subject almost every night. If there is no assignment in a particular subject, use the time you have scheduled for it to review and/or to revise class notes.

6. When you are beginning to study a new lesson or chapter, schedule extra time to read over notes from previous classes and chapters. This will enable you to better understand and appreciate how the new material relates to what you already know.

7. Budget your weekend time efficiently. Try to complete about 50 percent of the work on Saturday in order to avoid the traditional Sunday evening avalanche. Resist the temptation to see Sunday as Saturday's great labor-saving invention.

8. Plan to study for your most difficult courses during that time of day when you work most efficiently. If you are scheduling one long, continuous period of study, plan to deal with your hardest subjects first.

9. *Carefully plan* the use of your study periods and any unscheduled school time that might be available to you. This point is worthy of special emphasis because research has demonstrated quite conclusively that one hour of daytime study is equal to about an hour and a half of evening study. Work with your academic advisor or counselor on budgeting your use of blocks of unscheduled school time. Find places where you can usually be alone at the hours you are free. If on a particular day, your last class ends at 1:30, forget about breaking your personal record for getting home early. Remember that there is surely at least one place where you can study in the school building or on campus (frequently, the library), and that studying is the one activity you should be most concerned with during your peak-efficiency daytime hours. If the last few remarks seem especially annoying and strike you as being more of "the cruel and oppressive rhetoric of the slave-driving landlords of the educational domain," it is probably because you are both disturbed and offended by their glaring truth. Think about it!

10. Do not plan to change the study of one subject directly over to another subject similar to it. In other words, do not plan to study Latin after Spanish, or Chemistry after Mathematics, etc. (Perhaps it was the dull prospect of an evening's toil in only one type of subject matter that once led Mark Twain to quip, "Soap and education are not as sudden as a massacre, but they are more deadly in the long run.")

11. Keep copies of your schedule in your notebook, binder, or plan book and on your desk at home. If you have an organizer pro-

gram on your personal computer or a pocket organizer with sufficient space to store a weekly plan, enter your schedule there as well.

Chart 1								
a.m.	Mon.	Tues.	Wed.	Thurs.	Fri.	Sat.	Sun.	a.m.
12-6								12-6
6-7								6-7
7-8								7-8
8-9								8-9
Home Room Advisor								
Mod 2								9-10
3								
4								
5								10-11
6								
7								
8								11-12
9								
10								
								p.m.
11								12-1
12								
13								
14								1-2
15								
16								

17								2-3
18								
p.m.								
3-4								3-4
4-5								4-5
5-6								5-6
6-7								6-7
7-8								7-8
8-9								8-9
9-10								10-11
11-12								11-12

Chart 2

a.m.	Mon.	Tues.	Wed.	Thurs.	Fri.	Sat.	Sun.	a.m.
12-6								12-6
6-7								6-7
7-8								7-8
8-9								8-9
Home Room Advisor								
Mod 2								9-10
3								
4								
5								10-11
6								
7								
8								11-12

9								
10								
								p.m.
11								12-1
12								
13								
14								1-2
15								
16								
17								2-3
18								
p.m.								
3-4								3-4
4-5								4-5
5-6								5-6
6-7								6-7
7-8								7-8
8-9								8-9
9-10								10-11
11-12								11-12

* On both charts, "Mod 2" through "18" in the left hand column represent 20-minute units of time, running from 9:10 to 2:50.

Chances are that your school uses a different scheduling system. You should adapt this part of each chart to fit the schedule in use at your school .

Chapter III

Reading Speed and Comprehension

A. *Questions for Self-Evaluation*

Place a check mark in the column that you feel most accurately describes your own case now.

a. Rarely / Never

b. Sometimes

c. Often / Always

	a	b	c
1. Do I adjust my reading speed to suit the difficulty of the material?	___	___	___
2. Do I avoid saying the words under my breath as I am reading?	___	___	___
3. Even when I suspect that I have missed something, do I resist the urge to go back and re-read material I have already read?	___	___	___
4. Do I read some words on the printed page with greater care than I read others?	___	___	___
5. Do I use my hand to quicken my reading pace?	___	___	___

6. Do I quickly survey or glance over a
chapter or article before I begin a careful
line-by-line reading? _____ _____ _____

7. Do I remain interested in reading matter
by guessing ahead to what the author
will say next? _____ _____ _____

8. When I am reading material that is more
concerned with ideas than facts, do I locate
the topic sentences of paragraphs? _____ _____ _____

9. When I want to understand and recall what
I am reading, do I evaluate the material,
relating it to previously learned material? _____ _____ _____

10. Do I make use of signal words and editor's
clues when I am reading for main ideas? _____ _____ _____

11. Before I begin to use a textbook,
do I familiarize myself with the arrangement
and content of the entire book? _____ _____ _____

12. When reading and studying a textbook,
do I turn chapter headings into questions
and then read to answer my questions? _____ _____ _____

13. When reading and studying a textbook, do I pause at the end of a section to recite or state in my own words the material treated therein? _____ _____ _____

14. Do I make brief outline notes and/or underline my textbook as I am studying it? _____ _____ _____

15. When I have a large supply of outline notes, do I reduce them to a few pages of summary notes? _____ _____ _____

B. *Goals*

When you complete this chapter, you will

1. be aware of some ways to increase your reading speed;
2. appreciate the importance of adjusting your reading speed to the material you are working with;
3. know how to improve your comprehension and recall of material you are reading;
4. have a systematic approach to reading and studying textbooks (viz., the *SQ3R Method*).

C. *Reading Speed and Comprehension*

It is perfectly obvious that the ability to read with speed and understanding is the single most important factor in determining academic success. The reading assignments given to you in school will often be long and will frequently be dense, having a relatively large amount of information packed into a small amount of space. The point is that you cannot possibly allow the authors you are reading to elaborate their ideas at their own pace: you must attack the passages you are reading. If you think of reading assignments as mysteries, then you cannot afford the luxury of casually waiting around for the action to reach a climax. You must know the plot; at the earliest possible stage, you must know whether the butler did it. And if the solution to this mystery is going to have any great meaning for you, you must personalize it by reacting to it as it unfolds, according to your own values and background. This necessitates that you be an *active* reader, and that is exactly what most of the following suggestions are intended to help you to become.

General Observations on Reading Speed and Comprehension:

1. Your reading speed should suit the level of difficulty of the material. You can probably read *The Wit and Wisdom of a Faculty Member* at a rate of 400 words per minute (if a faculty member has 400 words of wit and wisdom!!!). But try reading *The Cohomology of Sheaves and Related Problems in Homological Algebra* at the same speed and you will soon find out whether the Dean has the good taste in office decoration that everyone claims. The reading process, then, should involve your conscious decision as to what reading speed enables you to achieve your objectives in each case. Is the material before you something you are eager to have thorough knowledge

of, or is it something that you only want to understand in a general way? In other words, should you read slowly and carefully, or should you read rapidly, hunting for main ideas and topic sentences?

2. Read articles or books that you are using in a supplementary role less deliberately than textbooks, great literature, or matter assigned in class. Read most slowly when you are dealing with scientific or highly technical material or poetry.

3. Avoid subvocalization (saying the words under your breath as you are reading). The lingering effect of reading aloud as children, vocalization makes it impossible to read rapidly because oral reading sets the upper limit of reading speed at the relatively low rate at which we speak.

4. Keep re-reading or regression, the conscious or unconscious movement of the eyes back over material already read, to an absolute minimum. Happily, this habit will give way to a conscious effort to avoid it. Always read easier material without stopping to puzzle out the meanings of sentences that are confusing or vague: later sentences usually clarify the points of previous ones. Of course, if the meaning does not become clear, you should re-read the obscure portions of the text. It is important, however, that you discipline yourself to re-read as rarely as possible.

5. The companion of an attack upon bad habits like subvocalization and re-reading is a positive reading objective. Your first goal should be to read groups of words rather single words. In a single line of an average book, you should attempt to

fix your eyes on two or three groups of words per line. This means that your eyes should focus upon three or four words in each group. To illustrate:

The eyes move	along the line	in three steps
from left to right	and repeat the pattern	line by line

As this practice becomes comfortable, you will establish a rhythm, quickly reading whole sentences and capturing the thought of the author.

6. Do timed exercises that force the pace of your reading beyond the rate at which you currently comprehend. You can use your right hand to pace yourself. Moving your hand along the lines from left to right, force your eyes to follow your hand. You should expect to lose comprehension at first, but in a short time, you will recover the same comprehension at a some-what higher rate of speed. Remember to practice at a speed that is slightly beyond your present capabilities, and do not surrender to the inclination to slow down. Keep a record of your performance.

7. Read a chapter or article over very rapidly once before you go about outlining or underlining. Without a broad view of the material you are dealing with, it is impossible to decide which portions of the text are most important; and the tendency in most students is then to outline or underline too much. This not only wastes your time, but also makes it more difficult

to conduct a quick review of important data before a test because too much matter has been designated as important.

8. Try to remain *active* and interested in the material you are reading by anticipating at every point what the author is likely to say next. When you have finished a paragraph or a section of a chapter, you should attempt to guess what ideas will follow. This is especially effective if you have already conducted a quick first reading and are in the process of a careful line-by-line reading. Under these circumstances, you are in a position to make educated predictions about what will come next, and you can more clearly perceive why and how what you have just read fits into the entire picture painted by the material you are reading.

9. When you are reading material that is more concerned with ideas than facts, it is good practice to underline the topic sentence in each paragraph (i.e., that sentence in each paragraph that you think best states what the whole paragraph is about, and to which all of the other sentences in the paragraph appear subordinate in meaning). Topic sentences are, in effect, main ideas in a chapter or article, and are in themselves an outline of the material.

10. When you strongly desire to understand and recall the material you are reading, it is generally a good idea to relate it to previously learned matter and to respond to the printed word in much the same way as you would respond to words used in a conversation. In other words, evaluate the meaning, accuracy, relevance, and implications of each new statement. What

does the statement mean? Can you think of any point that either proves or disproves the statement? Is the statement important? What does the statement lead you to conclude about other points made in the text? This type of mental exercise serves to paraphrase (that is, to summarize in different words) and review not only the statement in question, but also many of the other statements surrounding it.

11. When you seek to gain a quick comprehension of the main ideas in your reading, always utilize editor's headings, topics in boldface type, italicized words, and other highlighted material. Moreover, be on the lookout for signal words indicating the direction in which the author is taking his thought. Here are some examples of three important varieties of these signal words:

Words directing you to speed up your reading pace:

again	furthermore	moreover
also	in addition	more than that
and	likewise	similarly
	more	

Words directing you to slow down your reading pace:

although	however	on the contrary
but	in contrast	rather
conversely	in spite of	still
despite	nevertheless	yet

Words signaling you to carefully observe a summary
or conclusion:

accordingly	hence	so
as a result	in conclusion	therefore
consequently	in summary	thus

12. When you are reading or studying a textbook, take some extra
    time to understand graphs, diagrams, tables, or other illustra-
    tions that are intended to improve your grasp of the material.
    These visual aids are generally included for good reasons; they
    are not, as the architect Frank Lloyd Wright once described tele-
    vision, "chewing gum for the eyes."

A Specific Method for Reading a Textbook:

The following method for studying textbooks, created by F. P.
Robinson in *Effective Study*, is reprinted in its entirety from the
adapted form devised by C. Gilbert Wrenn and Robert P. Larsen in
Studying Effectively.[1]

---

1. Reprinted from *Studying Effectively* by C. Gilbert Wrenn and Robert P. Larsen. Copyright 1955 by Stanford University Press. Used by permission of the publisher. Adaptation
of *"Steps in the SQ3R Method"* from *Effective Study*, 4th edition by Francis P. Robinson.
Copyright 1941, 1946 by Harper & Row, Publishers, Inc. Copyright 1961, 1970 by Francis P.
Robinson. Reprinted by permission of the publisher.

The SQ3R Method

1. Make a hasty *survey* of your assignment to get the main ideas. This need not take more than two or three minutes. Note the title of the chapter; read any introductory, summary, and concluding paragraphs and leaf through the assignment to determine the main sections (generally three to six), thus getting the framework of the chapter. To begin reading your lesson without this bird's-eye view is like beginning an automobile trip without a road map or without knowing where you are going.

2. Turn the first heading into a *question*. This will arouse your curiosity and give you a purpose in reading. The question will make important points stand out while explanatory details, elaboration, and repetition are recognized as such. If there are no headings, ask questions that you think might be asked by your instructor.

3. *Read* to answer your question. This means that you read to the end of the headed section. Your rate of reading will depend on your purposes, the difficulty of the material, and your familiarity with it. While reading, make use of editors' signals (italics and boldface type), topic sentences, signal words ("first," "further"), and various summaries (including graphs and charts) to help you organize the material.

4. After you have read the first section, look away from your book and try briefly to *restate* the answer to the question. Use your own words and, if possible, give an example. If you can't give the answer, re-read the section. Then jot down cue

phrases in outline form in your notebook, particularly for later review. Make the notes brief. Now repeat steps 2, 3, and 4 on each succeeding headed section. That is, turn the next heading into a question, read to answer that question, restate the answer, and outline. Read in this way until the assignment is completed. Studies indicate that a quick review or restatement immediately after each reading period will insure almost 50 percent greater efficiency in remembering.

5. When your lesson has been read, *review* your notes to get a bird's-eye view of the various ideas and their relationships. Check your memory by covering up the notes and trying to recall the main points. Then, expose each main point and try to recall the subpoints listed under it. Further, you should always go over your outline just before a test. You tend to forget most of what you have learned during the first 24 hours. But remember that you can often re-learn in a few minutes what took you an hour to learn the first time.

In the beginning, the *SQ3R Method* may seem strange and difficult. However, after you become familiar with the method, it will result in a far greater mastery of your assignments, with no increase in time spent studying. It has five advantages: you are learning to distinguish between main ideas and details; you are training yourself to answer questions as you would on a test; you are reducing mind-wandering because you are making frequent checks; you are creating brief notes—using your own words—that prepare you more adequately for tests; and you are making the best possible use of the principles of memory.

There are several points that we would like to emphasize in connection with this method. Remember these four ideas:

1. Every study performed on the subject has demonstrated that outlining ideas on a separate sheet of paper is more effective than underlining or outlining in the margin of the textbook. Summarizing in this way is an activating process: it will get you involved in reacting to the material you are reading, and hence, will increase your ability to understand and absorb its meaning. Nevertheless, designating key words or sentences by underlines and writing marginal summaries are both acceptable study practices. The truly crucial point here, however, is that you should *always* have a pencil in hand and in use while studying a textbook.

2. It is *extremely* useful for you to familiarize yourself with the physical arrangement of the entire textbook. Read the preface, and use both the table of contents and the review section that may appear at the end of a chapter and that outline the main points you should know. As suggested in step #3 of the *SQ3R Method*, make maximum use of tables, graphs, drawings, pictures, maps, chapter headings, italics, and the like.

3. If you choose to use an outlining system, you will find yourself with a large quantity of notes to study for the final examination. Thus, it is always a good idea to pick out the most important points that appear in your outlines and to create three or four pages of compact summary notes.

4. When you are in the process of using the *SQ3R Method*, you will undoubtedly raise questions to yourself that your text-

book will not answer. Note these questions down and ask them of your teacher. Remember that he or she, too, is a vital educational resource ever at your disposal.

Chapter IV

Vocabulary and Spelling

A. *Questions for Self-Evaluation*

Place a check mark in the column that you feel most accurately describes your own case now.

a. Rarely / Never
b. Sometimes
c. Often / Always

a	b	c

1. When I come upon a new word in a reading assignment or during a class, do I check its exact meaning(s) in the dictionary? ____ ____ ____

2. Do I have a system for learning new vocabulary words? ____ ____ ____

3. Do I make a conscious effort to use my new vocabulary words in conversation and in writing? ____ ____ ____

4. Do I acquire some sense of what new words mean from the meanings of their various prefixes and roots? ____ ____ ____

5. Do I take care to correctly spell new terms
   and proper nouns when I write them
   in my notebook?   ____ ____ ____

6. Do I make an effort to apply a few basic rules
   of spelling when I come upon difficult or
   tricky words?   ____ ____ ____

B. *Goals*

When you complete this chapter, you will
1. have a systematic method for increasing your vocabulary;
2. be familiar with the meanings of particular prefixes and roots that commonly appear in the English language;
3. know a few fairly simple general rules of spelling which will help you spell many challenging words properly.

C. *Vocabulary and Spelling*

While it is true that having a good vocabulary will not necessarily propel you to the position of President of the United States or even to the exalted status of manager of the school Frisbee team, it is darn embarrassing to go through life unaware of exactly what people are talking about! Unless you are as wealthy as the famous moviemaker Samuel Goldwyn ("Include me out" and "An oral contract isn't worth the paper it's printed on," just to mention a few of his more curious statements), you will eventually come to appreciate the value of precise language as a vehicle of communication. In every endeavor, academic or otherwise, you will need both to express yourself clearly and accurately and to understand what others think they are clearly and accurately expressing to you. A good vocabulary, then, is vital to effective speaking and effective listening (in the academic world, writing and reading, respectively).

And similarly, unless you have the services of a stenographer who will take your notes for you, sit for your examinations, and write your papers, you will probably find it valuable to know how to spell the words you *want* to use. If nothing else, it will spare you wasted hours trying to think of apt synonyms that you *do* know how to spell.

Building a Vocabulary:

1. Whenever you come upon words with which you are unfamiliar, write them down on 3 x 5 index cards. On one side of the card, print the word itself, spelled correctly; on the other side, write the meaning(s) in legible form, and use the word in one or two sample sentences. Wait until you have noted 10 or 15 unknown words before you look up their meanings and write out the cards. Study the words on the cards at random moments.

2. Make note of all new words appearing in assigned readings, lectures, or class discussions. If a word is used that you *think* you understand because of the context in which it is used, make a note to check on its exact meaning. Look upon your teachers as a helpful resource for exposing you to new words and phrases; do not be afraid to ask them how to spell strange expressions.

3. Always try to use your new vocabulary words in written work and especially in conversation. The most important rule in vocabulary building is probably this: use it or you lose it!

4. Try reading the dictionary every now and again. You will probably be surprised at how interesting it can be, especially if you are free to skip around from page to page, word to word. Take a particular interest in derivatives (words formed by adding prefixes, suffixes, or both to a word or root), because in learning them you will actually be learning many other related words.

5. Remember that words are commonly composed of prefixes and roots. The following are the most common prefixes and roots in the English language, appearing in over 100,000 words.

Prefixes

Prefix	Variant Spellings	Meaning	Example
A-	An	without	amoral
Ab-	A-, Abs-	from, away from	absent
Ad-	A-, Ac-, Af-, Ag-, Al-, An-, Ap-, Ar-, As-, At-	to, toward	admit
Com-	Co-, Col-, Con-, Cor-	with, together	compete
De-	—	from, away from, down	depart
Dis-	Di-, Dif-	off, away from	distract
En-	Em-, In-	in, into	entrance
Epi-	—	over, upon, besides	epidemic
Ex-	E-, Ec-, Ef-	out of, from	expel

continued

Prefix	Variant Spellings	Meaning	Example
In-	U-, Im-, Ir-	into, not	insert
Inter-	---	between, within	interrupt
Intro-	Intra-	within	introvert
Mis-	---	wrong, wrongly	misconception
Non-	---	not	nonsense
Ob-	Oc-, Of-, Op-	to, toward, against	objection
Over-	---	above	overcast
Pre-	---	before	precede
Re-	Retro-	back, again	regain
Sub-	Suc-, Suf-, Sug-, Sup	under, below	submarine
Trans-	Tra-, Tran-,	across, beyond	transport
Un-	---	not	unfit

Roots

Root	Variant Spellings	Meaning	Example
Capt	Cap, Ceiv, Ceit, Cip	take, seize	capture
Ced	Cess	go, yield	concede
Duct	Duc, Duit, Duk	lead, make, shape	induct
Fer	Lat, Lay	bear, carry	transfer
Fic	Fac, Fact, Fash, Feat	make, do	fiction
Graph	---	write	autograph
Log	Ology	speech, science	dialogue
Mitt	Miss, Mis, Mit	send	transmit
Olic	Play, Plex, Ploy, Ply	fold, bend, twist	complicate
Pos	Pound, Pon, Post	put, place	depose

continued

Root	Variant Spellings	Meaning	Example
Scribe	Scrip, Scriv	write	prescribe
Sist	Sta	stand, endure	persist
Spect	Spec, Spi, Spy	look	inspect
Tain-	Ten, Tin	have, hold	attain
Tend	Tens, Tent	stretch, pull	extend

There are a host of common prefixes used to show number or amount. You should learn any of the following ones that you do not already know.

Prefix	Meaning	Example
Bi- (Bis)-	two	biannual
Cent- (Centi-)	hundred	century
Dec- (Deca-)	ten	decade
Hemi-	half	hemisphere
Milli- (Mille-)	thousand	millennium
Mon- (Mono-)	one	monotone
Multi-	Many, much	multitude
Octa-	eight	octopus
Pan-	all	panorama
Penta-	five	pentagon
Poly-	much, many	poly chrome
Prot- (Proto-)	first	prototype
Semi-	half	semi-finals
Tri-	three	triangle
Uni-	one	unification

6. Always be on the lookout for connections between the languages you are studying. Consider, for example, the remarkably great influences that Latin and Greek have had on English vocabulary, and you will immediately understand the value of observing similarities between tongues.

Latin Root or Prefix	Meaning	Example
Am	love	amorous
Anim	soul, spirit, breath	animate
Ante	before	anteroom
Aqu(a)	water	aquatic
Aud	hear	auditorium
Bene	well	benevolent
Circum	around	circumvent
Clar	clear, bright	clarity
Cord	heart	cordial
Corp	body	corpse
Cred	believe	credible
Digit	finger, toe	digital
Dom	tame, subdue	dominate
Don	give	donate
Dorm	sleep	dormitory
Fort	strong	fortitude
Frag (Fring, Fract)	break	fragile
Frat	brother	fraternity
Gen	begin, origin	engender
Jac (Jec)	cast	projection

continued

Latin Root or Prefix	Meaning	Example
Loc	place	locality
Nomin (Nomen)	name	nominate
Nov	new	innovation
Ped	foot	pedestrian
Per	through, by	perceive
Plen (Plet)	full	plentiful
Port	carry	portable
Post	after	postpone
Potent	able, powerful	potential
Pro	before	prologue
Sect	cut	dissect
Video	see	videotape

Greek Root or Prefix	Meaning	Example
Arch	chief, rule	monarch
Amphi	around, both sides	amphitheatre
Anti	against	antidote
Auto	self	automatic
Biblio	book	bibliography
Bio	life	biology
Cau (Caut, Cast)	burn	holocaust
Chron(o)	time	chronicle
Cosm(o)	order, arrangement	cosmic
Cirt	judge, discern	criteria
Dem(o)	people	democracy
Dia	across, through	diameter

continued

Greek Root or Prefix	Meaning	Example
Dyn (Dyna, Dynam)	power	dynamic
Geo	earth	geography
Hetero	different, varied	heterogeneous
Homo	same, equally mixed	homogeneous
Hydr(o)	water	hydrant
Macro	large	macroscopic
Mania	craze for	pyromania
Meter	measure	odometer
Micro	small	microfilm
Mor(o)	fool	sophomore
Nym	name	anonymous
Path	experience, suffer	sympathy
Ped	child	pediatrician
Peri	around	periscope
Philo	love	philosophy
Phobos	fear	claustrophobia
Phon(o)	sound	phonograph
Psych(o)	mind, soul	psychic
Scope	examine	stethoscope
Soph	wisdom	sophistication
Syn	together, with	synonymous
Tele	far, distance	telephone
Theo	God	theocratic
Therm	heat	thermometer

Based on just the prefixes and roots you have been given in this chapter, you should be able to determine the approximate meanings of hundreds of new words. Just to get you started in the right direction, see if you can work out a reasonable definition of any of these terms that is foreign to you.

Abduct	Circumlocution	Polytheist
Antecedent	Hydrophobia	Postscript
Antipathy	Impediment	Precept
Bibliophile	Incredulous	Replenish
Bisection	Monograph	Transpose

At this point one final word of caution might well be in order: while it can be great fun guessing at the meanings of terms based upon their component roots and prefixes, there is no substitute for the dictionary. To be sure you "know" what a word means, you really have to look it up. After all, if we used nothing but educated guesses and logic to arrive at definitions of terms, we would probably end up thinking that because lawyers are disbarred and clergymen defrocked, actors can be departed, ballplayers debased, cowboys deranged, dry cleaners depressed, electricians delighted, models deposed, musicians denoted, seamstresses dispatched, sleepers debunked, tree surgeons debarked, and perhaps even podiatrists defeated.

Improving Your Spelling

Nowadays because students so often do their written work on word processors equipped with spell check programs, it is important consciously to realize that misspellings are most likely to occur with homonyms (words sounding alike, but meaning different things and often spelled differently, as with "there," "their," and "they're") and proper nouns—neither of which the spell check feature will help you to catch. You yourself always have to proofread your work and check spellings in cases where you are at all uncertain.

Fortunately, it is relatively easy to learn how to spell new terms and proper nouns correctly: the best idea is to copy them into your notebook straight from your textbook or the board, being especially careful to spell them properly. This way, you will always be studying them as they should appear when they are written out. Unfortunately, the inconsistencies among commonplace nouns, verb, adverbs, and adjectives pose a more formidable challenge for the scrupulous speller. Even so, it would be foolish to give way to total despair. Although English spelling is riddled with irregularities and exceptions to general laws, there are a few key rules that, once known, will help you to spell hundreds of tricky words correctly.

Rule 1 "i" before "e" except after "c" or when pronounced like an "a" as in "weigh."

ie	ei (after c)	sounds like "a"
chief	ceiling	feign
niece	conceit	reign
thief	perceive	vein

Of course, there are exceptions to this rule, most of which are included in this sentence: "The leisured foreigners neither seized either species nor forfeited their weird heights."

Rule 2 Double the final consonant before adding a suffix that begins with a vowel if the word is accented on the final syllable and ends in a single consonant preceded by a single vowel.

Double	Single
occurrence	benefited (accent not on final syllable)
sitting	succeeded (preceded by two vowels)

Rule 3 In words ending in "y" preceded by a consonant, change the "y" to "i" before a suffix except one beginning with "i."
Flies (suffix is "es")
Flying (suffix "ing" begins with "i")

Rule 4 Drop the final "e" before a suffix beginning with a vowel, but keep it before a suffix beginning with a consonant.

Suffix with vowel	Suffix with consonant
coming	entirely
likable	hateful
refusal	movement
writing	ninety

One notable set of exceptions involves retaining the final "e" after "c" or "g" when the suffix begins with "a" or "o" (as in "courageous" and "noticeable").

And finally, to be absurdly specific, probably the single most frequently misspelled word in the English language is "separate." Note that there are only two "e"s and that there is "a rat" in "separate"; if nothing else, spare your teachers the thankless task of having to underline or circle this particular verbal nemesis.

Chapter V

Memory of Details and Factual Information

A. *Questions for Self-Evaluation*

Place a check mark in the column that you feel most accurately describes your own case now.

a. Rarely / Never

b. Sometimes

c. Often / Always

a	b	c

1. Do I study with the conscious intention of remembering what I am studying? _____ _____ _____

2. Do I have a relatively easy time selecting what information to commit to memory? _____ _____ _____

3. Do I perform memory work in short periods, resting my mind for a few minutes afterward? _____ _____ _____

4. Do I make an effort to understand material before I try to memorize it? _____ _____ _____

5. When I am memorizing large quantities of data, do I recite information aloud and/or write outlines of the material on a separate sheet of paper? _____ _____ _____

6. Do I try to memorize things in categories
or groups rather than in isolation?   _____ _____ _____

7. Do I have specific techniques or tricks
to memorize passages, vocabulary,
word combinations, and lists?   _____ _____ _____

8. Do I have a relatively easy time
memorizing numbers?   _____ _____ _____

B. *Goals*

When you complete this chapter, you will

1. have a basic understanding of the way your memory works;
2. appreciate the significance of oral reviews as a memory aid;
3. have a better sense of what information you should try to commit to memory;
4. be familiar with a number of specific techniques or tricks of memorization.

C. *Memory of Details and Factual Information*

In all probability, nothing is so crucial in the learning process as memory. After all, what benefit could you possibly gain from studying something if you were unable to remember anything about it? It is our hope that it will never be said about you what Richard Brinsley Sheridan, the late 18th-century playwright, once said about one of his enemies, that he was "indebted to his memory for his jests and to his imagination for his facts." Accordingly, we have devoted some of our attention to statements about memory and to suggestions of memory techniques—especially those statements and techniques that seem most immediately applicable to your academic needs.

Toward Developing a Better Memory:

1. Always study with the intention of remembering: this type of aggressive and positive attitude is bound to increase your attention and, hence, your ability to recall. Charles W. Eliot, the president of Harvard University for roughly 40 years, year-by-year recalled the names of students and faculty. He was motivated to do so by an embarrassing experience he had once suffered in failing to recall the name of one of his colleagues. In short, it helps to have an active interest in remembering.

2. Remember that the human memory is limited. In particular, the short-term memory is restricted in the quantity of information it can absorb. For this reason, it is important to spread out the exercise of your memory, that is, to use relatively short study periods that are separated by periods of mental rest. (So, for example, a 20-minute period might be followed by a 5-minute break.) Studies have consistently revealed that memorizing in a few short periods is more efficient than memorizing in one long period.

3. Remember that by reciting an idea aloud or by writing it down in outline form, and thus by keeping it in mind for four or five seconds, you can transform your recollection of that idea

from the temporary to the permanent memory. This is precisely why we have placed so much emphasis on oral review and written outlines in other sections of this booklet. Every review, no matter how brief, *dramatically* enhances the likelihood of recall. (Oral reviews are particularly effective because the material being memorized is heard as well as seen.)

4. *Be selective* in studying information that you wish to commit to memory. Obviously, you cannot recall every fact mentioned in a given chapter. If there are many facts within one paragraph, and you cannot decide which one to memorize, ask yourself which detail is *primary*. In other words, which fact is most closely related to the topic of that paragraph? Which is most clearly connected to the main idea?

5. Try to understand material before you attempt to commit it to memory. If you grasp the principles on which the information you are trying to recall is based, you are much more likely to recall it for a greater length of time.

6. Always remember the principle of association. Connect the material you are trying to recollect to anything in your own experience. Link this new data to any old bits of related information you already have. Attempt to relate what you are learning in one subject to what you are learning in others. The principle in effect here is that you are much more likely to recall the new information when you see it in some clearly defined context either from personal experience or *from previously learned* facts. *Be active* by using *what you already know*.

7. Remember that it is easier to recall a series of items if they are grouped in categories. Look for relationships between bits of information you are memorizing and then study the items under the headings suggested by those relationships. For example, rather than memorize a disorganized list of baseball players' names (such as, Mantle, Cobb, Gehrig, Schmidt, Mays, Clemens, Aaron, Musial, Ruth, and Bonds), learn them under those headings with which they are commonly associated (such as, American League: Clemens, Cobb, Gehrig, Mantle, Ruth; National League: Aaron, Bonds, Mays, Musial, and Schmidt).

8. If you are memorizing poetry or a passage of prose, repeatedly read several lines or sentences aloud at one time. Do not memorize single lines or sentences because, later on, you will find it difficult to recall the order of things. Generally, use the unit of sense (the stanza and the paragraph for poetry and prose respectively) as a guide to how much material you should read aloud repeatedly at each shot. This will reduce the problem of making transitions between the things you have memorized.

9. When you are memorizing many lines of poetry or a long prose passage, pick out key words in the text you are working with and underline them. Learn these key words first, in the order in which they arise in the material. Use these words as a memory outline upon which to hook the remainder of the matter you are seeking to recall.

10. Use acronyms (words formed from the first letters of successive words) to recollect particular combinations of words. So, for example, if you were trying to recall the names of four great NFL quarterbacks, you might order their surnames appropriately to come up with a single key word to remember, perhaps "FAME" to stand for Favre, Aikman, Marino, and Esiason. When confronted with an unvarying string of consonants, you can always insert what you know to be a few meaningless connector vowels. So if you were looking to recall who played whom in the Final Four semi-finals of a Grand Slam tennis tournament—say, Maria Sharapova vs. Martina Hingis and Lindsay Davenport vs. Venus Williams—you would try to remember the word "SHaDoW" and remind yourself that only the consonants have significance.

11. Use a flash-card system (explained in *Vocabulary*, *C*, *1*) to memorize English or foreign-language vocabulary, dates in history, formulae, etc.

12. If you wish to memorize a combination of ideas or a list of items, consider using the device of creating an absurd mental picture to enable you to unify the members of this series in your memory. Think of some silly picture or image to represent the first idea you are trying to recall. Rejoice in the fact that this is the rare case where being silly reaps big academic dividends because the more ludicrous the image you create, the more likely you are to recall it. Then, add one new ridiculous element to this original picture for each of the other phrases in the series or items on the list. Lastly, close your eyes for

a few seconds and visualize the final picture. (For example, suppose you were trying to recall this sentence from a newspaper article: "The United States and the Soviet Union sealed an atmospheric Nuclear-Test Ban Treaty in Paris in 1963." You might begin by picturing a bomb standing on its nose and in the shape of a roll-on deodorant stick. The word "Ban" is written on its side. Then, you might envision that there is a bear on one side of the bomb and an eagle on the other. Each one holds a leash connected to a seal that is sitting atop the weapon and is pushing it underground. To finish off the image, you imagine that the seal is wearing a beret that bears the date "1963" on its side. This picture is a bit ridiculous, but it is memorable, and every detail included in it represents some fact that you may want to recall.)

13. Probably the most difficult details to recall are numbers. Where an approximate recollection of numbers is sufficient because of their enormity (say, in memorizing populations of countries), numbers should be simplified, with numerical relationships being stripped down to simple ratios. If you are attempting to recall the relative size of City X, with its metropolitan population of 2,899,101, and City Y, with its metropolitan population of 1,404,688, simply memorize this: City X to City Y, 2 to 1.

14. Mark Twain once explained, "There are three kinds of lies: lies, damned lies, and statistics." Nevertheless, there are instances when the memorization of specific figures is totally demanded. When these occasions arise, here are a few specific suggestions on how to make the numbers more memorable:

a. One simple method for recalling a complicated series of figures is to devise a sentence in which the number of letters in each word represents one of the numbers in the series; of course, the order of the words in the sentence duplicates the order of figures you are trying to memorize. For example, suppose you were attempting to recall that the value of *pi* is 3.14159265. You might invent this sentence, "Yes, I have a large container of orange juice," and commit it to memory. Later on, you can easily recite the numerical value of *pi* simply by counting off the number of letters in each word.

b. Whenever you are trying to learn a series of numbers, look them over carefully to see if you can observe a pattern in them. Imagine that you were asked to learn the Social Security number 862-41-9375. Look at the figures to observe anything about them that might make the whole series more memorable. Do you see that every number from 1 through 9 appears in the sequence, but that no number is repeated? Do you see that all of the even numbers appear first, and that they are in decreasing value order except for the inversion of 2 and 4? Do you see that the odd numbers, the last five in the group, begin with the extremes (the lowest and highest, 1 and 9), and work downward (3 and 7) toward the numerical midpoint (5)? By studying the numbers in this way, you may be able to recall them without spending very much time reciting them aloud; if you forget one or two of them, you will probably be able to figure them out based on the patterns you observed.

c. Still another way to memorize a series of figures is to associate them with other numbers that have particular significance or greater "memorability" for you. Do any of the numbers you are studying bear any resemblance to phone numbers or dates in history you have already memorized? Do any of them translate into memorable dates (that is, days, months, and years, as the "41" in the middle of the Social Security number mentioned above can be converted into April 1 — a notable date indeed)? Do any of the numbers resemble test marks or grade-point averages you have recently scored (as the "9375" at the end of our Social Security number might remind you of your recent 93 in English and 75 in Chemistry)? Are any of the numbers more memorable if you think of them as life spans, batting or earned run averages, track times, golf or bowling scores, results of basketball games, numbers worn by your favorite players, or anything else? In short, what can you *associate* with these figures that once you think of it will allow you to recall the numbers you need to specify? Whatever it is, study it, and the numbers will readily come to mind.

Chapter VI

Taking Notes

A. *Questions for Self-Evaluation*

Place a check mark in the column that you feel most accurately describes your own case now.

a. Rarely / Never
b. Sometimes
c. Often / Always

	a	b	c

1. Do I take notes in all of my classes? ___ ___ ___

2. In group discussions, do I note down the best remarks made by my fellow students? ___ ___ ___

3. Do I read assigned material before the classes that will cover it? ___ ___ ___

4. Do I make note of only the more important information?

5. Do I take notes that are legible? ___ ___ ___

6. Do I take notes that are well organized? ___ ___ ___

7. Do I leave generous amounts of space in my
notebook to revise my notes after class? _____ _____ _____

8. Do I have a regular procedure for reviewing
notes that involves oral recitation? _____ _____ _____

9. Do I revise and review notes as soon as
possible after the class in which I take them? _____ _____ _____

10. Do I spend 20 or 30 minutes per week per
subject in reviewing my class notes? _____ _____ _____

B. *Goals*

When you complete this chapter, you will

1. understand the purpose of taking notes in class;
2. have a better idea of what information you should be sure to note;
3. know a method of taking down, organizing, and revising notes;
4. know when and how to go about reviewing your notes.

C. *Taking Notes*

There are at least three important reasons for taking notes in
class: first, they represent an efficient means of reviewing for examinations and quizzes; second, they help you to pay attention
during the class; and third, their writing forces you to impose an
order upon the remarks that you are hearing in class and enables
you to grasp relationships between ideas even as you are listening

to the lecture or discussion. The last two points are especially important to bear in mind because, as we have suggested so many times up to this point, it is crucial that you be *active* in the learning process. You simply cannot expect your teachers to learn for you: the degree of your involvement in a lecture or discussion is the only measure of what you have gained from it.

Specific Suggestions on Taking Notes:

1. Take notes in *every* subject. Be prepared to note not only remarks made during formal presentations by the teacher, but also ones offered during small-group discussions. Often, your fellow students will have some excellent things to say that will help you to better understand the subject under discussion. As suggested above, taking such notes will insure that you pay close attention to what is being said; moreover, it will increase your motivation to participate in discussions.

2. Be sure to read assignments before class. You will discover that it is much easier to organize your notations of the teacher's remarks if you already know something about the subject.

3. Be *active* and energetic in taking notes. Do not be a passive receiver of information who simply copies down a few of the exact words the teacher utters. Restate the material the teacher is presenting in your own words, and evaluate the information as you are writing it down. (What you desperately want to avoid is the kind of "lecture" situation where information passes from the notes of the teacher to the notes of the student without passing through the mind of either.)

4. Be *selective* in taking notes. There is plainly no need to take down everything the teacher is saying. Try to determine what the *main* ideas of his or her presentation are, along with the *major* examples or pieces of evidence he or she is presenting in support of them. Pay particular attention to remarks made in a louder voice or at a slower pace than normal. Try to listen to the full explanation of ideas or concepts before you begin writing anything down. Copy into your notebook all diagrams, drawings, tables, and other illustrations the teacher puts on the blackboard. Take everything down in a way that is complete enough and legible enough to make ready sense later on.

5. Use a system of numbers and letters to organize the teacher's comments. Have these signify the major divisions and subdivisions of his or her presentation. There are countless ways to do this, but here is one arbitrary illustration:

I. American League
   A. Eastern Division
      1. New York Yankees
         a. pitchers

6. There is no need to perfect an elaborate system of shorthand in order to take good notes. Instead, you might simply glance over the following list of ideas and adopt those that suit your particular needs:
   a. Omit "a" and "the."

b. Omit unimportant verbs.

is

be

went

c. Use symbols for common connecting words.

& = and

w/ = with

w/o = without

== results in, leads to

vs.= against

∴= therefore

d. Use mathematical symbols where they are appropriate.

≠ = does not equal

a > b = a is greater than b

a < b = a is less than b

f = frequency

e. Omit periods in standard abbreviations.

eg = for example (from the Latin *exempli gratia*)

ie = that is (from the Latin *id est*)

dept = department

CIA = Central Intelligence Agency

f. Use only the first syllable of a word.

col = colony

dem = democracy

rep = representative

g. Use all of the first syllable and only the first letter or two of the second.

comp = comprehensive

ind = individual

subj = subject

h. Eliminating final letters, use just enough of the beginning of a word to recognize it easily.

ach = achievement

info = information

intro = introduction

transp = transportation

i. Omit vowels from the middle of words, keeping only enough consonants to recognize the word immediately.

bkgd = background

maj = majority

pkgd = packaged

spt = sport

j. Use an apostrophe where appropriate.

am't = amount

gov't = government

k. Form the plural of an abbreviated word by adding "s."

chaps = chapters

rivs = rivers

l. Use only a "g" to stand for "ing" endings.

decrg = decreasing

exprtg = exporting

wlkg = walking

m. After you have fully written out a name or title a first time, use only its initials when you refer to it again. (Write out

"National Labor Relations Board" the first time you refer to it, but "NLRB" in all subsequent references.)

7. It is wasteful to completely rewrite your notes. Make them usable as you are writing them down by leaving generous amounts of space in the margins and at the bottoms of pages. One convenient method for increasing the usefulness of your notes is to leave about 2½ or 3 inches of space in the left-hand margin. When the lecture or discussion is over, you can then go back to provide marginal summaries of the information that clarify and organize ideas.

8. Whether you are taking notes by hand or making use of a laptop, always use the left-hand margin as a review or recall column. Place headings or concise summaries in this space when you review your notes after class. When you are finished making this marginal outline of the lecture or discussion, cover the main column and, using your jottings in the review or recall column, state the facts and ideas mentioned in the class as you remember them. Make questions out of your marginal headings in the same way that you were urged to do with headings in textbooks. Next, uncover the main column to determine the accuracy of your oral recitation of the material covered in class. This procedure, intended to activate you in the process of learning, is a key to fastening information into your long-term memory.

9. Study your notes *as soon as possible* after the class in which you take them. Probably the single most important period for long-term recall of information is the time shortly after your

first exposure to it. Every study on memory indicates the overwhelmingly positive impact of this type of immediate review: it will double or triple the amount of data recalled weeks after the class, and will make review for major examinations a remarkably easy task. Thus, it is critical that you allocate at least 20 or 30 minutes per week per subject for review of recent class notes.

Chapter VII

Participating in Class Discussions

A. *Questions for Self-Evaluation*

Place a check mark in the column that you feel most accurately describes your own case now.

a. Rarely / Never

b. Sometimes

c. Often / Always

a	b	c

1. Do I participate freely and openly in class discussion? ____ ____ ____

2. Do I carefully read and think about assigned materials before coming to class to discuss them? ____ ____ ____

3. When others are speaking, do I listen for ideas rather than just facts? ____ ____ ____

4. Do I listen carefully when the teacher or discussion leader explains the topic and rules or guidelines of the discussion? ____ ____ ____

5. Do I try to look at whoever is speaking as much as possible? ___ ___ ___

6. Do I note down especially good comments soon after they are made? ___ ___ ___

7. Do I speak aloud only after thinking for a few seconds to insure that my remark is worth voicing, thus avoiding the temptation to over-participate? ___ ___ ___

8. Do I reflect on other students' ideas rather than accept them at face value? ___ ___ ___

9. Do I try to build on good points suggested by other students and address my reactions to the people whose thoughts provoked them? ___ ___ ___

10. Do I try to apply what others are saying to myself and to find ways to connect their remarks to previous discussion topics and readings? ___ ___ ___

11. Do I try to anticipate where the discussion is going even while it is in progress? ___ ___ ___

12. Do I ask questions when I do not understand something? _____ _____ _____

13. Do I ask my questions during pauses or natural breaks in the class? _____ _____ _____

14. When asking questions and making comments, do I vocalize so that everyone can hear them? _____ _____ _____

15. Do I consciously try to phrase my comments during discussions in terms that are clear, concise, complete, and concrete? _____ _____ _____

16. Do I consciously try to avoid using clichés, popular sayings, and sweeping generalizations? _____ _____ _____

17. Do I try to provide specific examples to illustrate the point I'm making? _____ _____ _____

18. Do I try to avoid becoming defensive or overly aggressive when my opinion differs from those of others? _____ _____ _____

19. Do I try to respond to what others say sensitively and sincerely, reacting according to what is said rather than who says it? _____ _____ _____

20. Do I know enough to drop the argument
when I find myself repeating my ideas before
an unconvinced majority? ____ ____ ____

21. Do I listen to others with special interest
and note down any conclusions that the
teacher or discussion leader draws at the
end of the class? ____ ____ ____

22. Do I review these and my own conclusions
later that day? ____ ____ ____

B. *Goals*

When you complete this chapter, you will

1. appreciate some of the advantages of participating in
   class discussions;
2. know how to improve the quality of your participation;
3. have a better understanding of how to gain the most knowledge that you can from a class discussion.

C. *Participating in Class Discussions*

Most of the courses you take in school will naturally involve some
degree of class participation. In many subjects, most notably
Math, Science, and Modern and Classical Languages, you will be
expected to supply relatively brief responses to in-class questions
and perhaps to write solutions on the blackboard. In other subjects, however, such as English and Social Studies, you will be

expected to take an active part in group discussions. The purpose of this chapter is to permit you to gain the most out of classes of the latter type.

In-class discussions are difficult for many students because they are, by nature, public events. If you study hard for and do well on a test, chances are that nobody will label you a "teacher's pet"; if you say something laughably outlandish on a paper or examination, chances are that you will not be subjected to open ridicule. On the contrary, when you make yourself visible to all by asking questions and volunteering comments during group dialogues, you run certain risks, two of which have already been implied. Indeed, there is safety in the kind of mentality espoused by former President Calvin Coolidge, who once reasoned, "If you don't say anything, you won't be called on to repeat it."

What, then, does this mean? Does it mean that you should not offer remarks or ask pertinent questions while classes are in progress? Certainly not!

But why *should* you participate? Here are four of the more obvious reasons:

1. Instructors often use their impressions of the nature and extent of your class participation to gauge your effort and the sincerity of your interest in their subjects. Sometimes, discussion participation represents a specific percentage of your grade, but in almost every course it has *some* bearing upon your ultimate performance, because it is such a glaring index of your desire to learn. And being human, teachers can hardly

help but give the benefit of the doubt and provide extra help to someone who plainly wants to understand material and who generously seeks to share his or her perceptions about it with classmates.

2. Class meetings represent the ideal time to resolve problems in understanding. A good question raised when material is being treated during class can clarify in moments an issue that may take hours to grasp when doing homework or preparing for a test. And a purposeful and interesting class discussion can prompt dozens of new insights that make the connections between different ideas, or between facts and ideas, infinitely clearer, that make the subject itself more interesting, that make the data more memorable, and that make related essay questions on future examinations seem more like gifts than evaluations.

3. Asking questions and participating in group discussions will enliven the class meeting for you and make time seemingly breeze by. If anything, you should be most eager to participate in those subjects that you find least appealing: "tuning out" will only make you more conscious of how time is dragging by.

4. Even if you ask an occasional silly question or offer a remark that either the teacher or your peers feel is fruitless, you have little to lose. Your ego is certainly strong enough to endure criticism or even a laugh at your expense. The odds are overwhelming that whatever you said will be forgotten by the time the next period begins. And if it isn't, so what? Even the ablest thinkers in the class have volunteered foolish remarks

here or there, and think of all the intelligent insights that would have been lost if they had allowed themselves to be discouraged to the point of silence. Besides, in a good discussion your classmates are thinking themselves; they are not sitting there waiting to pounce on the smallest slip of your tongue. And if they are, either they respect you immensely or they have more to be embarrassed about than you, no matter how preposterous your comment. (We all naturally tend to imagine that everyone's attention is simply riveted on us, when, in reality, this is almost never the case. Can you recall, for example, the time before last that your two or three best friends gave incorrect responses when the teacher was calling on students around the room? Probably not—and remember, these are your close friends. On the contrary, you probably can vividly recall the last five errors you made under the same circumstances, and you may well imagine that everyone else can too. Humanity is sometimes an unwittingly egocentric lot!)

Assuming that you are now resolved to ask questions and participate in discussions when the opportunity arises, here are some concrete suggestions on what you should do.

Specific Suggestions for Discussion Participation:

1. Carefully read all of the assigned material before you come to class. Note down any questions you may have about the subject matter and think about its contents. Jot down in your notebook what you felt were the main ideas it presented. Re-

member the political philosopher Edmund Burke's comment: "To read without reflecting is like eating without digesting."

2. Above all else, try to be a good listener. This involves paying close attention when the teacher or discussion leader explains the topic that is to be considered and establishes boundaries and procedures for the dialogue. It also involves listening for ideas and not just facts, looking at whoever is speaking as much as possible (and depending in part upon the type of seating arrangement being used), and noting down particularly good ideas advanced by the teacher or your classmates, preferably after they have finished speaking (and before the speakers after them get deeply into their points). The American writer and philosopher Henry David Thoreau was certainly correct when he noted, "It takes two to speak the truth—one to speak, and another to hear." If you are disposed to do so, you can learn as much or more from a discussion than you can from a lecture, and if you listen attentively you are likely to find yourself forming an abundance of worthwhile, original thoughts that you will want to share with your peers. If you tune out, you may well become caught in that awful position of being called on to react to or summarize what other students are saying. If this situation comes to pass, you will likely end up sympathizing with President Coolidge, who, when asked by reporters what a particular clergyman preaching on the subject of sin had said to the congregation, could only reply, "He said he was against it."

3. Think before you speak. Never volunteer an observation unless it is an improvement over silence. Sometimes, the first thoughts that shoot into our minds *seem* so brilliant and profound that we almost cannot resist blurting them out aloud; be wary of these "insights," for no sooner are they vocalized than they seem ridiculous. (Some examples of recent educational vintage include the following: "Happily, he lived until the day he died," "It's dog eat dog out there or the reverse," and "People are human.") You *do* want to participate, but you don't want to become known as the Yogi Berra of your class ("I want to thank you for making this night necessary," "You can observe a lot just by watching," and "Nobody goes there anymore; you can't hardly get a seat" are just a few of his more famous extemporaneous remarks). And you *don't* want to deny others the opportunity to contribute to the discussion by virtue of your over-participation.

4. Look for opportunities in the discussion to make *helpful* contributions. Try to build on good comments made by other students, if possible directing words to the person whose remark or question inspired your reaction. (Usually, teachers prefer to guide the dialogue, not manipulate it, and they often prefer that students speak to one another, especially within a circular or semi-circular seating arrangement.) When someone makes a statement, do not accept it at face value: think about it carefully and consider any implications in the language that was used to phrase it. As the discussion is in progress, apply whatever points

other students are making to your own experience, and look for intelligent ways to connect their observations to previous discussion topics and especially to assigned readings. When there is a lull in the discussion, volunteer any important conclusions you have reached in either of these regards. Finally, while you are listening to others speak, try to anticipate where the discussion is going, what ultimate findings it is pointing toward. This can be done rather easily, since most people say only about 100–150 words per minute and your ears and mind can take in somewhere over 400, and it will help you to pay *closer* attention and contribute later observations.

5. Ask questions when teachers come to pauses in their presentations, and when there is a momentary break in the conversation during class discussion. Ask the question so that everyone, not just the teacher, can hear it; the odds are very good that other students are puzzled by the same point you are and that most of your peers would benefit from hearing the answer. Listen to the entire answer before you raise any follow-up concerns, but do not be afraid to say that you are still confused even after hearing the explanation.

6. When you volunteer remarks during class discussions, follow these guidelines:

a. speak loud enough for all to hear; be clear and to the point (unlike the Hungarian foreign minister who Mussolini said "took a long running start to jump over a straw"), but use sentences rather than short phrases;

b. use concrete language to the extent that you can ("My brother has the flu" is considerably more expressive than "Someone I know has a problem");

c. try to avoid resorting to tired old clichés or simple-minded aphorisms, which are either meaningless or convey different meanings to different people ("out of sight, out of mind," for example, if translated into a foreign language and then back into English, would probably come out to be something like "invisible maniac"); and

d. if possible, give a specific example or two to illustrate your point, since your conclusions will not be as persuasive as your reasons for arriving at them.

7. At all costs, avoid making sweeping generalizations—especially close-minded, negative ones that make discussion impossible (as in "Anyone who likes poetry should be shot," or "Everyone over 25 is a jerk," and so on). And if you are challenged on a particular point, do not become so defensive that you start boasting of your own ignorance (like the famous criminal Al Capone, who, when asked about Canadian liquor he was bootlegging into the United States during Prohibition, playfully replied, "I don't even know what street Canada is on").

8. As the discussion unfolds, defend your views forcefully but not too aggressively. As the old Chinese proverb says, "Do not use an axe to remove a fly from your friend's forehead." In other words, by being tactful in responding to other students' arguments or in disagreeing with the teacher, you make your points without making enemies. Be sensitive to the feelings

and opinions of your peers; do not emulate W. C. Fields, who rather callously advised a fellow complaining of insomnia that he should "get plenty of sleep." At the same time, be sincere enough not to agree automatically with any word spoken by your best friend just because he or she is your best friend; never tell someone he or she is "open-minded" when you actually think he or she has "a hole in his or her head." And finally, know when to drop a point. When you find yourself repeating the same ideas and phrases a second time, and the majority of people *still* disagree with you, you should abandon the point in contest. If what you said the first time around did not persuade them, it is not likely to do so when reiterated without new and stronger arguments. Always remember these words of Franz Kafka when you find yourself upholding an unpopular position: "In a fight between you and the world, back the world!"

9. Listen with particular care to any conclusions that the teacher or discussion leader draws at the close of the dialogue. If he or she asks for help in forming them, by all means volunteer; but if he or she is obviously pressed for time as the class is ending and does not ask for aid, quell any desire you may have to speak. Write down what the speaker says and record any important conclusions of your own that have been omitted from his or her summation. If you run out of time, dig out your notebook again during your first free period or later on that day when you are reviewing what went on in class. Re-evaluate these conclusions of the group in the light of your own views.

Chapter VIII

Taking Tests

A. *Questions for Self-Evaluation*

Place a check mark in the column that you feel most accurately describes your own case now.

a. Rarely / Never

b. Sometimes

c. Often / Always

a	b	c

1. Do I have a positive attitude about tests in that I regard them as challenges? ____ ____ ____

2. Do I compete only against myself (my past performances) and not against others on tests? ____ ____ ____

3. Do I know the type of test (objective or essay) that I will be taking and prepare accordingly? ____ ____ ____

4. Do I follow a pre-arranged schedule for review before major examinations? ____ ____ ____

5. Do I avoid having to "cram" (studying large quantities of new information for an extended period of time) shortly before tests?   _____ _____ _____

6. Do I get a good night's rest prior to examinations?   _____ _____ _____

7. Do I arrive at the examination room early and have all materials I will need to take the test?   _____ _____ _____

8. Do I motivate myself to work hard in preparation for tests by planning some reward for my efforts when they are over?   _____ _____ _____

9. Do I carefully read all directions before I begin a test?   _____ _____ _____

10. Do I know the precise meanings of words used in the directions on examinations?   _____ _____ _____

11. Do I bring a watch to tests and plan out the division of my time between questions?   _____ _____ _____

12. Do I avoid running out of time
on examinations?   ____ ____ ____

13. On objective tests, do I skip questions
I cannot answer immediately and come back   ____ ____ ____
to them later on?

14. On objective tests, do I read every question
in its entirety?   ____ ____ ____

15. On objective tests, do I pay special attention
to the way questions are worded?   ____ ____ ____

16. When time permits, do I carefully review
my answers to objective questions before
handing in my paper?   ____ ____ ____

17. Do I prepare for essay tests by anticipating
likely questions and planning out
answers beforehand?   ____ ____ ____

18. On essay examinations, do I try to stick to
the topic as much as possible and avoid
lengthy introductions?   ____ ____ ____

19. On essay examinations, do I pay
particular attention to neatness,
organization, and coherence?   ____ ____ ____

20. Do I re-read my essay responses before handing in my paper? ____ ____ ____

21. When I have a choice of essay questions, do I answer the ones I know best first? ____ ____ ____

22. When I have a choice of essay questions, do I very rapidly decide which ones to do, selecting ones that will not overlap in the content of their answers? ____ ____ ____

23. Do I refuse to be discouraged by a poor test performance? ____ ____ ____

24. Do I know how to handle the situation when my teacher has made a mistake or been unfair in grading my examinations? ____ ____ ____

25. Do I review examinations in preparation for the next test? ____ ____ ____

B. *Goals*

When you complete this chapter, you will

1. have a better attitude about tests and a greater understanding of what they represent;

2. know certain general principles that should govern the way you prepare for and take all examinations;

field events than baseball or basketball: you are competing against your own best time or distance, rather than against other competitors.

3. Try to learn the type of examination that you will be taking. Remember that objective (short-answer) tests usually measure your ability to *recognize* information, whereas essay tests evaluate your ability to *recall* and organize information. Thus, you should review a greater quantity of material, while committing less information to memory, in preparation for an objective examination. On the contrary, you should emphasize oral recitation and memory work in preparation for essay tests.

4. Arrange a schedule for review. Be somewhat selective in determining what to review. Use a condensed or summary outline of the material you will be tested on in order to provide yourself with a general view or a sense of "the big picture." Remember that writing such summaries is itself a form of review.

5. Realize once and for all that "cramming" will work if and only if the information under study has *already been learned* (and that is not really "cramming" at all). If the material you are working with is altogether new and undigested, cramming results in confusion and, as every study on the subject has conclusively indicated, in an incredibly low rate of recall. In a word, cramming large quantities of new data into a pressured and overworked brain will prove to be about as useful as waxing the car just before the demolition derby.

6. Try to get a typical night's sleep before you take a major exam.

7. Arrive at the examination room a few minutes early so that you do not feel rushed at the beginning of the test. Of course, you should arrive prepared, having pens, paper, and any reference material you may consult during the examination.

8. Establish in your mind some reward for your dutiful preparation for the test. This is best done one or two days before the examination. Think of this reward shortly before you begin the test.

9. If you feel nervous at any point during the examination, or just before you begin, close your eyes and take a few deep breaths to help you relax.

Taking Objective Tests (Multiple Choice, True/False, Sentence Completions, and Matching Columns):

1. Read all of the directions on the test first. Be sure that you understand everything that the examination calls for you to do. Ask the teacher about procedure now.

2. Determine whether there is a penalty for incorrect guesses. This, of course, dictates whether it is logical for you to guess. (And if there is no penalty, *guess* at all multiple choice and matching column questions. Even a broken clock tells the correct time twice a day!)

3. *Budget your time*. If there is an essay question on the examination, determine how much time you should devote to it based on its point value and its difficulty. As you are answering the short-answer part of the test, check your watch from time to time to insure that you are moving at a rate rapid enough to allow you the time you need for the essay. (Needless to say, this means that you should have a watch!)

4. As a rule, skip those questions that you do not know the answer to immediately, and come back to them later on. This is to insure that you have a sufficient amount of time to get to all of the questions you know. Place a mark in the margin indicating that you have omitted a question. This will help you to locate it when you return to answer the questions you have skipped.

5. Read every question *in its entirety*. In multiple choice questions, read every choice option before you decide upon the correct answer. If you cannot immediately decide on the correct answer, draw lines through those options you can eliminate.

6. Where possible, change confusing words into simpler form. For example, you should alter the double negatives in a statement that reads, "It is not incorrect to say that Evelyn and Carl Lewis were not unsuccessful sprinters." By translating successive negatives into positives, you would create, "It is correct to say that Evelyn and Carl Lewis were successful sprinters."

7. Be attentive to the level of generality used in a question. There are particular words, sometimes referred to as qualifiers, or clue words, that are essential to your proper interpretation of the question. These would include the following:

all	always	more	best	can
every	invariably	equal	better	may
each	often	identical	good	must
many	usually	less	bad	should
most	occasionally		worse	would

continued

some	seldom		worst	
few	rarely			
none	never			

8. On sentence completions (fill-in questions), if you cannot recall the precise phrasing used in the text or by the teacher, use concise synonyms of your own. You may earn partial credit.

9. Remember that all parts of a compound multiple choice option (one choice having separate ideas linked by a conjunction) must be correct for that option to be the correct answer to the question. Similarly, all parts of a compound statement in a true-false question must be true for the answer to be "true."

10. Be systematic in doing matching columns. Begin at the top of the left-hand column and compare the initial item in the right-hand column. Continue to read down the right-hand column until you locate the correct choice. Then go to the second item in the left-hand column and repeat the process. Do the ones you are sure of first, crossing out entries in both columns that you have used.

11. Time permitting, go back to re-read all of the questions with an eye toward carelessness. Do not change your answers unless you have a good reason. First impressions are usually more accurate than second thoughts. Unfortunately, there is some quality in human nature that leads us, when we have time to think about it, to prefer the alternative we did not choose over the one we did; this is why the line other than the one we are standing in always seems shorter. Stay

in the same line unless you definitely recognize that it is the wrong one.

Taking Essay Tests:

1. Be active in preparing for tests by anticipating what questions are likely to be asked and by planning out your answers beforehand. Do not simply prepare for one or two possible questions. Be thorough, and do not merely hope that you will "luck out" on the day of the examination. Remember this saying of Ben Franklin: "He that lives upon hope will die fasting."

2. Read directions to questions with great care. Be certain that you are interpreting the question accurately, and that your essay answer addresses the question. To insure your understanding of those terms most frequently employed as directions to essay questions, we here provide a list of their general definitions:

Analyze — examine in detail, separating the subject into its parts to study their nature and interrelationship.

Comment — explain, analyze, or illustrate the subject at hand.

Compare — examine two things for qualities they have that resemble each other, emphasizing similarities, but mentioning very broad differences.

Contrast — examine two things for qualities they have that differ from each other, emphasizing the uniqueness of each, but alluding to broad similarities.

Criticize — indicate your conclusions about the truth or accuracy of some judgment expressed in the question, explaining the reasons for your findings whether they agree or disagree.

Defend — present and justify the arguments in favor of something.

Define — give a clear, concise, and documented meaning of some thing, omitting details but establishing the precise range of the thing being defined.

Demonstrate — make evident by reasoning and examples; show through the use of logical analysis and factual proof.

Describe — characterize, or relate in logical sequence.

Diagram — present a drawing, chart, table, plan, or some other graphic answer; label diagrams clearly and include brief explanations or descriptions where needed.

Discuss — carefully examine or analyze, giving detailed reasons pro and con, but arriving at some clear conclusion.

Enumerate — devise a list or state in outline form, presenting points concisely, one by one, in their logical order.

Evaluate — carefully examine or analyze some idea or subject stated in the question, emphasizing both its pros and cons in the light of factual evidence and expert opinion, and minimizing your own opinions.

Explain — make clear and understandable by presenting the meaning of and reasons for something, stressing major causes of important results.

Illustrate — use a picture, diagram, or specific example to explain or demonstrate something.

Interpret — translate, illustrate, solve, or take a personal position on a particular subject.

Justify — present and defend the arguments or reasons for something, making sure to use convincing examples.

List — devise an itemized series of points, using concise enumerated statements.

Outline — set up a description of something under main points and subpoints, overlooking minor details and emphasizing the arrangement of things.

Prove — show that something is the case by providing appropriate factual proof and clear logical reasoning.

Relate — indicate how things are connected to each other, or how one thing causes another, blends with another, or resembles another.

Review — analyze a subject in detail, presenting ideas and opinions about the topic within some broad logical pattern.

State — present all of the main ideas in brief, clear sequence, overlooking details and specific examples unless you are explicitly asked for them.

Summarize — provide the main ideas or facts in abbreviated form and in their logical order, overlooking details and examples unless you are specifically asked for them.

Trace — describe in paragraph form the progress of some process, its point of origin to its conclusion.

3. Stick to the topic as best you can. Keep directing the focus of your essay answer toward what you know, for, as Will Rogers once put it, "Nothing is so stupid as an educated man if you get him off the subject he is educated in."

4. Write as neatly and as legibly as you possibly can. As a rule, it is probably wiser to sacrifice length for appearance. Few essay

responses, no matter how thorough, are likely to earn high grades from a squint-eyed and bespectacled instructor who is forced to study them as though they were hieroglyphics. *Always* allow time to re-read your essay answers for their legibility and for errors in spelling, punctuation, sentence structure, pronoun usage, subject/verb agreement, etc.

5. Pay special attention to organizing your essay answer in a highly logical sequence that a reader might easily follow. Subconsciously, teachers are sometimes as readily influenced by the organization of a response as they are by its content. To illustrate the point, if you were asked to specify what letters are used to spell "champ," you would be likely to receive a higher grade for spelling "chump" than for spelling "mhpac"; even though the second spelling is more accurate because it contains all of the letters in "champ," it is likely to earn a lower grade because the order of the letters is unrecognizable, making it look more wrong than the alternative. Because organization is so crucial, it is plainly worth a few minutes of your time to create a very brief outline before you begin writing your essay response.

6. Use transitional words and phrases between ideas to maximize the coherence and fluency of your essay answers. The following is a list of transitional words and expressions along with their corresponding significations:

Type of Relationship	Transitional Words and Expressions
Admission	admittedly, accepting the fact, granting that, of course, true
Cause and effect	accordingly, as a result, because, consequently, for this reason, hence, since, thus, therefore, if ... then
Development or extension of thought	at the same time, also, for example, in addition, in other words, likewise, moreover, similarly, that is, too
Emphasis	above all, add to this, besides, even, more, indeed, more important, most significant
Increasing quantity	also, besides, furthermore, in addition, moreover, too
Order	at this point, first, finally, last, next, second, then
Reversal of thought	albeit, but, conversely, despite, however, in another sense, nevertheless, on the contrary, on the other hand, still, though, yet
Summary	for these reasons, in brief, in conclusion, in short, in summary
Time	afterward, at last, at length, after this, before, currently, formerly, from now on, henceforth, later, meanwhile, now, once, presently, previously, since then, soon, subsequently, then, thenceforth, thereafter, ultimately

7. Avoid long-winded introductions. Begin your essay answers with several concise sentences that summarize what your entire essay is going to be about. Psychologically, it is good for the reader to feel from the very start that you know what you are doing. Moreover, should you run short of time, the reader

knows where you would have taken your ideas had you not run out of time.

8. If you are at a loss to answer a particular question, begin by writing whatever information you do have. (Whatever you do, try not to push the panic button by starting to shovel any old written garbage. You must know *something* concrete about the subject. And try not to sit there doing nothing but getting frustrated and angry with the teacher. Pleasant fantasies about plastering your teacher with a Boston cream pie should be reserved for another occasion.) Possibly, as you are in the process of spelling out this data, additional information will be called back to mind. If you are still at something of a loss for words, project or reason to conclusions based on the partial data you have. This procedure is not unethical as long as you are sincere in your attempt to reason to this "guessed" information. After all, as Samuel Butler once noted, "Life is the art of drawing sufficient conclusions from insufficient premises."

9. Do not trouble yourself to write "Time" or "No Time" at the conclusion of an unfinished answer. The teacher will presumably realize that you do *not* want to conclude in mid-sentence.

The following observations are related to essay examinations that require more than one essay response:

1. If you have a choice of questions, very quickly decide which ones you will answer. Always plan out your use of the time available to you based on the point values of the questions. Obviously, if you are to answer two questions of equal point

value, where the degree of difficulty does not vary enormously, it is best to divide your time equally between them.

2. In general, it is wise to answer an essay question you know more about before one you know less about. Do not "save the best for last," because you may not have sufficient time to present "the best" as effectively and as thoroughly as you can and want.

3. Do not hesitate for a long time on a problem question. Try to use the associative method suggested above (#8). When this fails, go on to the next question. Remember to resist your inclination to go on "shooting the bull," and recall with some fondness Mark Twain's explanation for the impossibility of some types of problems: "There ain't no way to find out why the snorer can't hear himself snore."

4. Leave space after each essay answer. This way, if you have time at the end, you can go back to add some additional information that you may have overlooked or forgotten in your original response.

5. Choose to do essay questions that overlap minimally in the content of their answers. In other words, if you are asked to write two essays, each one dealing with any two of the 45 novels you have read so far in your English course, do not write both answers on the same two novels. Remember that your objective on essay tests is to impress your teachers with the startling range of your knowledge (or, perhaps more accurately, to conceal from them the still *more* startling range of your ignorance).

Test Return:

1. Do not allow yourself to grow too discouraged by a bad performance, especially if you feel as though you labored hard in preparation for the test. Remember this saying of the great French writer Francois Rabelais: "Row on, no matter what happens."

2. Bear in mind that there is little practical advantage in complaining about the difficulty of an examination. Remember that everyone took the same examination, and chances are that at least some students scored fairly well. Remember, too, that teachers fully expect students to object to examinations and attach little weight to informal protests lodged by a few students who fared poorly.

3. Never argue over any point about which there is the slightest possibility of error on your part. You will earn only the teacher's anger and your fellow students' resentment. Check out the point first; if you are right, then consult the teacher.

4. Never point out computational errors or other obvious mistakes in correction during an in-class review of a test. Likewise, do not be too headstrong in debating judgment calls in the grading of your examination if the forum is a public one. Teachers have at least one similarity to umpires and grizzly bears: while they are normally rather passive creatures, if you back them into a comer, they are likely to rear up and fight.

5. If you firmly believe that the teacher has been unfair or inaccurate in grading one of your essays, the best thing to do is to ask the teacher to re-evaluate your response. Indulge yourself neither in heated argument with your teacher over the

matter, nor in the all too frequent outside-of-class stream of nasty and insulting anti-teacher remarks. The first method is likely to fail; the second, even while immediately satisfying, will definitely fail.

6. Keep all of your examinations. Read them over carefully, making sure that you understand exactly where you went wrong. (You might even re-work mistakes in red ink when you first get a test back in order to make later review easier and more helpful.) Ask yourself what you should have done differently to prepare for the examination. Before you take your next test in the same subject, pull out old tests to remind yourself of how and what you should study, to figure out how to avoid making similar mistakes on the upcoming test, and to plan what your strategy should be as you are taking the examination.

3. have a strategy and techniques for taking objective examinations;

4. have a strategy and techniques for taking essay examinations;

5. be more aware of how to evaluate and react to examinations when they are returned.

C. *Taking Tests*

If there is one thing that any reputable school can promise its students over the course of their academic careers, it is that they will be bombarded, torpedoed, and otherwise assaulted with a seemingly unending barrage of examinations and quizzes. Surely, students must sometimes feel like members of the 18th-century Admiralty in England — a place about which the French writer Voltaire once observed, "In this country, it is good to kill an admiral from time to time to encourage the others." Indeed, it would be no less than ridiculous for us to explain to you the importance of the pages that follow.

General Observations on Taking Tests:

1. Develop a positive attitude toward examinations. Regard each test as a challenge to be met. If you are troubled by unsuccessful past performances, remember that it is not how you start off in a course that counts, but how you finish.

2. Compete, but compete only against yourself and your past performances, not against others. You want to achieve a performance level that is good for you, without regard to other students' performances. Examinations are more like track and

Chapter IX

Writing Papers and Essays

A. *Questions for Self-Evaluation*

Place a check mark in the column that you feel most accurately describes your own case now.

a. Rarely / Never

b. Sometimes

c. Often / Always

a	b	c

1. Before I begin to write a paper or essay, do I fully grasp the requirements of the assignment? ____ ____ ____

2. When given a choice, do I choose to write on subjects in which I have an interest? ____ ____ ____

3. Do my papers and essays have a unifying thesis, that is, one topic or argument that serves as a focal point for the entire assignment? ____ ____ ____

4. When I have selected a topic to write on, do I ask the teacher's opinion of it before I begin writing? ____ ____ ____

5. Whenever I copy quotations or ideas from books or articles, or borrow material from the Internet, do I consistently and clearly indicate my use of the sources? ____ ____ ____

6. When I use material from the Internet, am I careful to verify the accuracy of that material, as well as the reliability of the Web site source? ____ ____ ____

7. Before I begin to write, do I discuss the topics of my papers and essays with others? ____ ____ ____

8. When I am working on word processor software (Word, WordPerfect, etc.), do I save my file frequently and make a back-up copy, either on a separate drive or disk, or by emailing it to myself? ____ ____ ____

9. Do I write quick first drafts of my papers and essays, forgetting temporarily about spelling and grammar? ____ ____ ____

10. Do I then read my first drafts aloud, checking them for all types of errors, especially those not caught by spelling or grammar checks? ____ ____ ____

11. Do I ask others to read my first drafts
and point out ideas or sentences that
may be unclear?   ____   ____   ____

12. Are my papers and essays clearly and
logically organized?   ____   ____   ____

13. Are my papers and essays unified
and coherent?   ____   ____   ____

14. Do paragraphs in my papers and essays
include topic sentences that summarize
the main ideas of the paragraphs?   ____   ____   ____

15. Do my papers and essays include
distinct and effective introductions
and conclusions?   ____   ____   ____

16. Do I review my teachers' corrections on
papers and essays to determine how I can
improve my performance?   ____   ____   ____

B. *Goals*

When you complete this chapter, you will

1. have a better understanding of what a paper or essay should
be concerned with;

2. have a better understanding of what a paper or essay should accomplish;

3. have a clear grasp of how a paper or essay should be organized;

4. be familiar with a systematic procedure for writing a paper or essay.

C. *Writing Papers and Essays*

In the immortal words of Dr. Samuel Johnson, the great writer, lexicographer, and all-around sage, "What is written without effort is in general read without pleasure." The function of this chapter, then, is to provide you with a few suggestions on directing your compositional labors. We presume that you recognize the importance of writing good essays and papers, if for no other reason than to "please" the teachers who read them and who respond with "pleasant" grades.

Suggestions on Writing Papers and Essays:

1. Be sure that you fully understand the requirements of the assignment. If you have any doubts, ask the teacher personally.

2. If some measure of choice is allowed, select a subject area in which you have an interest and can write about sincerely. Insincerity will almost always reveal itself in a paper. For this reason, it is important that you be honest and straightforward about the subject and that you do not feel an obligation to make flattering or complimentary remarks about the subject that you do not really mean. (Shun the "Hollywood Style" as

you would the measles. You should never find yourself making statements like the following in an essay: "Since the dawn of time, man has dreamed of expressing the kaleidoscopic rainbow of emotions that surge in his heart. In *The Scarlet Letter*, that dream has finally become an ecstatic reality." Once you write something even vaguely resembling this, you have lost credibility forever!)

3. On most assignments, it is desirable to have a unifying thesis, that is, one proposition or argument that is the dominant concern of your paper. This thesis is stated clearly at the beginning and is then defended throughout the rest of the paper. It is your main idea or "topic."

4. Once you have decided on your topic, it is a good idea whenever possible to test the waters on your instructor's opinion about it. Does he or she think it is a suitable topic to write on? Does he or she think that you will be able to treat the topic fairly and thoroughly within the page length required by the assignment? (Never choose a topic that is so broad that it cannot be dealt with adequately within your paper. Keep making your topic more and more specific until it can be treated sufficiently well within the allowed space.)

5. Determine if you should (or are) permitted to perform outside research for the paper. If you are required or elect to do outside reading, be careful not to commit "plagiarism," the improper use of someone else's original ideas and/or particular language. These days especially, the ready access you have to information through the Internet increases the temptation

to cut and paste intellectual and scholarly material and pass it off as your own. However, finding information on the Internet, repackaging it, and submitting it as your work is every bit as dishonest as copying from an uncited print source. Moreover, such copying does nothing to advance your educational growth, which is the very purpose of your school assignments in the first place. Remember that the penalties for plagiarism are very often quite harsh, and can include a failing grade for the course (not just for the assignment itself), academic suspension, or even expulsion. The simple solution for avoiding plagiarism is to properly cite and credit all the sources that you use, be they book, article, or Web site. When in doubt, cite your source!

6. If in doing research you have relied heavily on information drawn from an Internet source, cross-check the facts where possible and establish the credibility of their provider. Since you are ultimately responsible for the evidence and information in your essay, it is important that you make smart decisions when it comes to selecting which Web sites to treat as "authorities" in your own work. What follows in the next two sections are helpful guidelines for distinguishing useful sites from those that are potentially unreliable.

7. One of the easiest ways of identifying an unreliable Web site is if the site does not provide a list of its sources. If you cannot determine where the site is getting its information, then it is probably smarter to avoid treating it as an authority. In a similar vein, be wary of those sites whose authorship is also

vague. If an author is unwilling to take credit for his or her work, it is often a sign that the material is not worthy of becoming part of your own scholarly work. However, just because a site lists its sources and authors does not mean you should necessarily feel confident in the veracity of its material. If most of the content from *Joe's Guide to World War II* comes from Joe's grandfather (who loves to tell war stories), you probably want to search for a more authoritative source for information. Likewise, a report that states cigarettes are actually good for you might not seem so reliable once you realize the report was written by a major tobacco company. In short, then, before using a Web site as a source make sure to identify its author and sources and (to the extent possible) determine their credibility and impartiality.

A slightly different type of Web site that you should also be particularly wary of is *Wikis*, or collaborative Web sites that allow any user to make changes to material on the site. Increasingly, students have turned to these sorts of reference pages because they provide information on a seemingly endless range of topics. However, because any user (including yourself) could edit that information, there is no guarantee that any (or all) of the material is factual or impartial.

Furthermore, because *Wiki* pages are constantly being edited, they pose an additional difficulty in providing a static link for your citation. While *Wikis* are often fine sites to find other, more factual sources (check their citation sections), they should not be used as proxy for an old-fashion book or article. Finally, before relying on any information from a Web site, try to determine when the site (and material) was last updated. Even reliable Web sources can be behind on the times, so double-check to confirm that their information is both current and correct.

8. In light of the above dangers, it might seem fairly impossible to find reliable material on the Internet. However, there are an enormous number of factual (and valuable) Web sites out there that can greatly benefit your research. One of the simplest ways to identify safe sites is to ask your school or public librarian. Often, libraries create indexes of excellent research sites, as well as provide access to certain research databases that are closed to individual users. More often than not, these sites alone are enough to fulfill the average student's research needs. In addition, you might also consult sites such as Google Scholar, a search engine designed to limit its results to scholarly articles and journals. While these types of search engines are far from perfect, they tend to provide a more reliable set of research sites from which to draw information. Finally, you can in fact use information from less academic sites, provided that you take the time to double-check and confirm the information that you find there. This is a calculated risk on your part (of course, the information could still be wrong!), but cross-checking facts will help weed out the more outlandish information.

For the above reasons, the Internet should be treated as a wonderful, but imperfect resource for you as a student. The availability of more information to you nowadays implies your responsibility to sift and evaluate, to separate the wheat from the chaff, and to discern what is accurate, balanced, and insightful. In that respect, the Internet has only made your job as a student all the more challenging!

9. Make arrangements to have others assist you in the composition of your paper. Before you begin to write, discuss your subject area and topic with a friend, a member of your family, or your advisor or counselor. When you have completed a first draft of the paper, ask someone else to read it with an eye toward identifying sections of the assignment that may be unclear or confusing. (Ask anyone who will do it: even a grandmother can tell what does not make sense to her! Do not be so self-satisfied with your own writing as is one of the characters in an Oscar Wilde play who remarks: "I never travel without my diary. One should always have something sensational to read in the train.") Demand an honest reaction, and do not be put off when you get one, even if it is as unkind as Dorothy Parker's famous remark about some unfortunate author's work: "This novel is not to be tossed lightly aside, but to be hurled with great force."

10. Once you begin to write a first draft, do not stop. For the time being, forget entirely about spelling, grammar, and everything else your English teacher has probably been browbeating you about. You can deal with these concerns later on. For now, just write, skipping lines and leaving plenty of margin space. If using a word processor program, double space, so that

when you print out a hard copy later on, you'll have plenty of room to edit your work. Keep in mind, however, that when working on a computer, it is ALWAYS a good idea to "save" your text intermittently—certainly every page or so—and to make a back-up copy of your work on a separate disk or drive. (In fact, it might even be prudent to make a back-up of that back-up by emailing it to yourself!)

11. Carefully review your completed first draft for errors in spelling, pronoun usage, disagreements in number, punctuation, sentence fragments and run-ons. If you are working on a word processor, at this point spell check and style check programs can be helpful (though they are no substitute for actually editing the documents yourself). In addition to these practical concerns, you should also check that your work has variety in terms of sentence type and length, avoids clumsy or ambiguous phrasing, and especially possesses coherence. Does one sentence lead logically into the next? Does one paragraph flow logically into the next? Do transitions or links need to be added at various points?

12. Always read your corrected draft aloud before creating your final version of the assignment. Many errors are apparent to the ear but not to the eye.

13. As suggested above, word processing and desktop publishing are terrific assets when it comes to writing and editing a paper. They also give you the ability to produce a professional looking document. Remember, though, appearances are not the same thing as substance: a rose may look and smell bet-

ter than a cauliflower, but it does not make a better soup! While a computer can help you generate a document that seems sophisticated and complete on its surface, it does not do the thinking for you or provide insights when you have none. Desktop publishing, specifically, is a tool that can be used to incorporate charts, graphs, artwork, and photographs into your own work. Such illustrations should be used selectively and in the precise context of what you have to say. They are meant to clarify, augment, or emphasize points that arise in the natural development of your thesis, and, no matter how sharp they might look, are of no particular value in and of themselves. Choose graphics and create formats based on how effectively they support communication of your specific ideas, and do not get caught up in visual "bells and whistles" that your instructor will likely see through in a flash.

14. The latter point notwithstanding, appearances definitely do count for something! The final copy of your paper should be as error-free as you can make it, but should show no signs of the editing that went into making it so. It should be clean, neat, and inviting to the reader's eye; fair or not, there is a subconscious impulse in any grader to assume that more thought and effort went into something visibly polished. Studies show that where the content of two papers is relatively equal on their merits, the attractive, more readable document will generally yield the higher grade. Take heart from the fact that even Dr. Johnson, the great English stylist quoted at the beginning of this section, was once told by one of his college

tutors, "Read over your compositions, and wherever you meet with a passage which you think is particularly fine, strike it out." (That his ego readily withstood such severe criticism is perhaps best demonstrated by his later delight in tearing into the written efforts of others. He told one aspiring author, for example, "Your manuscript is both good and original; but the part that is good is not original, and the part that is original is not good.")

15. If you fare poorly on a paper, do not be discouraged. Review the instructor's corrections with an eye toward how you can improve your performance in the future.

Overall Organization of Papers and Essays:

1. Introduction—The introduction can be a single sentence or several paragraphs. Its purpose is to indicate the subject of your paper and to interest your reader in the topic at hand. Often, the introduction provides valuable background material and explains the division of the arguments presented in the paper. The introduction usually begins with more general observations that narrow down to the statement of some specific thesis (a main idea), which the more general remarks have indicated the worth of developing. The movement of the introduction, then, is from the general to the specific.

2. Body—The body of the paper is composed of those paragraphs that provide evidence or arguments in support of your main idea and that refute evidence or arguments that appear to disprove it. These paragraphs should, of course, be arranged

according to the logical sequence of their topics (the order in which the various paragraphs should be developed for your main idea to seem both clear and reasonable), and should contain numerous concrete details and specific examples that prove your main idea. Transitional words and phrases (ones that extend or reverse the previous thought, such as those listed in Chapter VIII) should be used to connect sentences within the paragraph. The first sentence of each of these paragraphs should include a clear and distinct topic sentence, which states the main idea of the whole paragraph and to which all other sentences in the paragraph are subordinate. The last sentence in the paragraph should provide a transition into the next paragraph.

3. Conclusion — The conclusion is normally a summary statement of the major ideas of your paper. It is neither the place where you grew tired of thinking, nor a mere restatement of the introduction; rather, it is an attempt to explore the implications of your main idea now that its truth and accuracy have been demonstrated. In a word, it should state the basic idea of your paper in some different and relatively striking way. It usually begins with the specific topic and then broadens itself to include the more general significance of that topic (i.e., how your main idea fits into some larger and even more important picture). The movement of the conclusion, then, is from the specific back to the general.

A Step-by-Step Procedure for Writing Papers and Essays:

1. Decide upon a precise topic for your entire paper.

2. Place the topic within a broad context and define any major terms that require such definition. This is, in effect, your introduction.

3. Decide upon topic sentences for all of the paragraphs that will be included in your paper. Translate the relationships between these sentences into words and phrases. (These will serve as the bases for transitions between paragraphs later on. Expressions such as *"The next point," "In contrast to this opinion," "To further support this idea,"* or *"On the other hand, Ruth also knew ..."* are only a few examples of how words can be used to link new paragraphs to previous ones.)

4. Decide what concrete details and specific examples relate most closely to each of the different paragraphs (i.e., according to their topic sentences).

5. Translate the relationship between the details and examples in each paragraph into words and phrases. (These will be your transitions between sentences later on. Again, see the list of transitional expressions in Chapter VIII for some examples.)

6. Write the paragraphs that compose the body of the paper, paying attention to the order of the paragraphs, the order of the information within paragraphs, and the transitions between ideas that you have determined in steps 3, 4, and 5, respectively.

7. Revise what you had earlier created as your introduction (step 2) based on what you actually say and prove in the body of the paper.

8. Write a conclusion that summarizes and broadens the implications of your topic. (You may prefer to write a rough version of the conclusion immediately after creating a rough version of the introduction, if only to clarify exactly what must be done in the body of the paper in order to prepare for the grand finale.)

Chapter X

Using Advisors and Counselors

A. *Questions for Self-Evaluation*

Place a check mark in the column that you feel most accurately describes your own case now.

a. Rarely / Never
b. Sometimes
c. Often / Always

a	b	c

1. Do I immediately bring my academic problems to the attention of my advisor or counselor? ___ ___ ___

2. Do I inform my advisor or counselor of personal problems that may be affecting my academic performance? ___ ___ ___

3. When my advisor or counselor is passive in relating to me, do I take the initiative in communicating? ___ ___ ___

4. Do I try to keep my advisor or counselor informed of my general academic progress, my extracurricular participation, and my overall frame of mind? ___ ___ ___

5. Do I listen to the advice my advisor or
counselor offers to me?   ____ ____ ____

B. *Goals*

When you complete this chapter, you will

1. better understand how to use your advisor or counselor;
2. recognize the responsibility you have to keep your advisor or counselor informed about academic concerns.

C. *Using Advisors and Counselors*

Ever feel so abused that you wonder if your teachers have been grading your tests and papers while having lunch at Burger King because they are so smeared with a rich red substance? Ever feel so depressed about your social life that you think you could walk on snow without leaving even a momentary impression? Ever feel so down about things in general that the whole world seems like a tuxedo while you're a pair of brown shoes?

Well, believe it or not, that funny-looking person with the milk of magnesia in the top right-hand drawer of his or her desk, whom you know as your faculty advisor or counselor, really is there to help you work through these and similar problems. Even though he or she probably knows next to nothing about contemporary music and still regards the Atari as "the only true gaming system," this person has had a considerable amount of experience in most areas where students have problems. Most faculty advisors and counselors, in fact, have been "hanging out" at one school or another since they were tots themselves. Virtually no problem that you can bring to such people will surprise them.

Remember that faculty advisors and counselors, the lifeguards, so to speak, in your academic swim of existence, have different attitudes toward your health and well-being. Some will always be swimming immediately behind you, pulling your head out of the water every time you start to go down for the first time; others will remain ashore waiting for you to call out for assistance should you need it. But no matter what position advisors and counselors take with respect to you, they are all willing to come rushing to your aid. You need only remember that it is largely your responsibility to notify such a person when he or she is needed and to warn him or her of those occasions when to keep a special eye out for a potentially drowning you.

There are at least five obvious occasions when you should quickly initiate contact with your advisor or counselor:

1. when you are having problems motivating yourself to do schoolwork;
2. when you are doing poorly in a subject or do not understand the bulk of the material, despite having already seen the teacher for extra help;
3. when you are having personal difficulties that are affecting your motivation and academic performance, including problems involving your parents, teachers, peers, or romantic partners;
4. when you suspect that your commitment to extracurricular activities, either in school or in your neighborhood, is adversely influencing your scholastic progress;

5. when you feel depressed about things in general and do not have a clear idea about why you feel this way.

Generally, though, you can be fairly certain that you should seek the aid of your advisor or counselor whenever you get a negative answer to this question: "Do I feel that there is a close connection between how hard I am studying and the kinds of grades I am achieving?" While you should certainly inform the appropriate teachers about your "no" response to such a query, you should also immediately hustle off to see your counselor or advisor, who can be of the greatest assistance to you when the problem is detected in its early stages. Whatever you do, do not wait until your counselor or advisor gets around to seeing you in the natural course of things; by that time, your sense of frustration will have mounted and failure might almost be a mathematical certainty. Not much good can come when you send the advisor or counselor a desperate message from your academic Alamo saying, "Wish you were here!"

In your regular or informal meetings with your advisor or counselor, keep him or her abreast of your overall academic situation. Let him or her know if you are having difficulties in a subject and could benefit from having a tutor. Mention any non-academic or personal circumstances that you feel could ultimately influence your scholastic performance. Volunteer information about your participation in extracurricular activities. Be open with the counselor or advisor, and always do your best to be communicative in his or her company. In short, make friends with this person, seeking out his or her advice in all matters that you feel comfortable sharing with them.

And when the advisor or counselor gives advice, listen!!! Even students who welcome conversation and invite counsel too often adopt the attitude that says, "I'd sure like to know what you think," but means, "I'll listen to what you have to say provided it doesn't interfere with what I've already decided." Avoid making the same discovery that Mark Twain did as he grew older, leading him to remark, "When I was 14, 1 couldn't stand to have the Old Man around; by the time I was 21, I was amazed at how much the Old Man had learned."

Conclusion

It is our hope that the observations and suggestions we have made in the previous pages will prove valuable to you. In closing, we can only remind you of your responsibility—your obligation—to evaluate them and to try them out with an open mind.

To be sure, you are a capable and talented individual. But despite your native abilities, you need to discipline yourself to the task of performing hard work; in other words, you must train yourself to study efficiently, and thus to become a genuine student. Knowing the best way to go about studying is at least as important as your IQ. And knowing how to learn is more important in the end than *what* you learn, because knowing how to learn will bring you toward the achievement of whatever overall goals and ultimate objectives you yourself set for your education.

In fact, Thomas Alva Edison, a fellow not altogether without instinctive and creative intelligence, may well have been correct in remarking, "Genius is one percent inspiration and ninety-nine percent perspiration." If you take the recommendations of this book to heart, you may rest assured that you are at least working up a high-efficiency sweat!

Frank Walsh holds a B.A. from Manhattan College and an M.A. from Fordham University, both in English. He was elected a member of Phi Beta Kappa in 1971. He has taught English at Fordham University and Regis High School, where he currently serves a member of the Guidance Department.

Chris Reisig is a graduate of Harvard University; he is currently a teacher of Literature and American Studies at Regis High School in New York.

* * *

Regis High School was founded by the Jesuit Order in 1914 as a tuition-free, independent college preparatory school. Throughout its history it has selected its students on a competitive basis from among the most talented young men in the New York metropolitan area. Regis has its roots in the 450-year tradition of Jesuit education and seeks to blend the sound features of contemporary educational research and practice with the perennial values of its tradition.